MY ÁNTONIA

The Road Home

TWAYNE'S MASTERWORK STUDIES

Robert Lecker, General Editor

MY ÁNTONIA
The Road Home

John J. Murphy

TWAYNE PUBLISHERS • BOSTON

A Division of G. K. Hall & Co.

My Ántonia: The Road Home
John J. Murphy

Twayne's Masterwork Studies No. 31

Copyright 1989 by G. K. Hall & Co.
Published by Twayne Publishers
A Division of G. K. Hall & Co.
70 Lincoln Street, Boston, Massachusetts 02111

Copyediting by Barbara Sutton.
Book production by Janet Z. Reynolds.
Typeset by Compset, Inc. of Beverly, Massachusetts

Printed on permanent/durable acid-free paper
and bound in the United States of America.

Library of Congress Cataloging-in-Publication Data

Murphy, John J. (John Joseph), 1933-
    My Ántonia : the road home / John J. Murphy.
        p.   cm. — (Twayne's masterwork studies ; no. 31)
    Bibliography: p.
    Includes index.
    ISBN 0-8057-7986-8 (alk. paper). — ISBN 0-8057-8035-1 (pbk. :
alk. paper)
    1. Cather, Willa, 1873-1947. My Ántonia. I. Title. II. Series.
PS3505.A87M8945   1989
813'.52—dc20
                                             89-2136
                                              CIP

In memory of
Margaret Shadegg Murphy
(1909–1986)
cook
and
Mary Ann McGahern Shadegg
(1882–1964)
storyteller

Contents

A Note on the References and Acknowledgments

Many readers of Willa Cather have contributed to this volume in influencing my reading of *My Ántonia*. Most of these will go unmentioned because they are the students I have taught over the years at Brigham Young University, Merrimack College, and the College of Saint Teresa. From those who are acknowledged I must single out Mildred Bennett of the Willa Cather Pioneer Memorial and Marilyn Arnold of Brigham Young University, the first for her tireless efforts in discovering and preserving the raw materials of Cather's art and the second for professional support as well as her careful and exhaustive bibliography of criticism on Cather. Others who have helped include Patricia Phillips of the Willa Cather Pioneer Memorial, who deciphered the Pavelka letter, and Ann Billesbach of the Willa Cather Historical Center, who provided the photographs of Cather and Annie Pavelka and their milieu. I have benefited also from conversations about Cather with Bruce Baker and Susan Rosowski of the University of Nebraska, and David Stouck of Simon Fraser University. Most of all, I thank Kevin Synnott of Russell Sage College for his insights on Cather and for providing me with a place in New England to think through this project, and my wife Sally, who typed the manuscript and pointed out where the writing failed to say what I intended it to.

The texts used throughout the commentary include Houghton Mifflin's 1961 Sentry Edition of *My Ántonia* and L. P. Wilkinson's 1982 translation of Virgil's *The Georgics*, Penguin Books, with commentaries by Wilkinson. All critical views incorporated into my commentary on *My Ántonia* have been acknowledged in chapter 3. For chapter 4, I am indebted to the Bennett, Bohlke, and Woodress volumes, as indicated in the initial paragraph.

Portrait of Willa Cather
Nebraska State Historical Society

Chronology:
Willa Cather's Life and Works

1873   7 December, Willa Cather (named Wilella after her father's youngest sister) born in Back Creek Valley (Gore), Virginia. First child of Charles Cather and Mary Virginia Boak Cather.

1874   Charles moves family to Willow Shade, his father's sheep farm, after William and Caroline Cather (Willa's grandparents) visit their son George in Nebraska.

1883   In April the Charles Cathers, now including sons Roscoe and Douglas, second daughter Jessica (three other children were born in Nebraska), and Willa's maternal grandmother, Rachel Boak, join William and George and their families in the Catherton precinct of Webster County, Nebraska.

1884   In September Charles moves his family to Red Cloud, the county seat, to open a loan and insurance office, and rents a house at Third and Cedar. Willa develops life-long friendships with members of the Miner family and meets Annie Sadilek, the prototype of Ántonia Shimerda in *My Ántonia*.

1890   Willa graduates from Red Cloud High School, delivers the commencement speech "Superstition *versus* Investigation." Moves to Lincoln in September to prepare to enter the University of Nebraska, matriculating as a regular degree candidate a year later.

1891   Essay on Thomas Carlyle, Willa's first appearance in print, published in March in the *Nebraska State Journal*. Switches from science to humanities as her major course of study. Develops friendships with Dorothy Canfield Fisher and Louise Pound.

1892   Has short story "Peter" published in Boston magazine *The Mahogany Tree* in May.

1893	Begins writing column "One Way of Putting It," which includes dramatic criticism, for the *Nebraska State Journal* in November.
1895	Graduates from University of Nebraska in June, returns to family in Red Cloud.
1896	In January short story "On the Divide" published in the *Overland Monthly,* the first time Cather's work appears in a magazine of national prominence. Moves to Pittsburgh in June to edit the *Home Monthly* and later begins reviewing for the *Pittsburgh Leader.*
1897	In September begins job as the day telegraph editor for the *Leader.*
1899	Meets Isabelle McClung sometime during the spring.
1901	Moves into the McClung family home. Begins teaching English and Latin in Pittsburgh high schools.
1902	Spends summer in Europe with Isabelle McClung and meets British poet A. E. Housman.
1903	Publishes first book, a collection of poems, *April Twilights,* in March.
1905	Publication of short story collection *The Troll Garden,* containing "Paul's Case" and "The Sculptor's Funeral," in March.
1906	Moves to New York in May to join the staff of muckraking *McClure's Magazine,* later serving as its managing editor (1908–11).
1908	In February, while on assignment in Boston for *McClure's,* meets Annie (Mrs. James T.) Fields, the widow of Hawthorne's publisher, and Sarah Orne Jewett, Maine local colorist, an important influence on Cather's fiction. Takes apartment in New York with fellow Nebraskan Edith Lewis, who continues to live with Cather until her death in 1947. Friendships develop during the *McClure* years with writer Elizabeth Sergeant and playwright Zoë Atkins.
1911	Takes a leave of absence from *McClure's* in September to spend three months with Isabelle McClung in Cherry Valley, New York, where she revises her first novel, *Alexander's Bridge,* writes "The Bohemian Girl," and begins "Alexandra," eventually a part of *O Pioneers!.*
1912	*Alexander's Bridge* begins serialization in February and is published as a book in April. From April to June Cather travels in the Southwest for the first time and explores cliff dwellings of

the Anasazi. Returns to New York via Nebraska and visits the Bohemian settlement in Webster County.

1913   *O Pioneers!* published in June. Cather meets opera singer Olive Fremstad and begins *The Song of the Lark.*

1915   Visits Mesa Verde, Colorado, with Edith Lewis in August. *The Song of the Lark* is published in October and dedicated to Isabelle McClung.

1916   Isabelle McClung marries, and Cather visits the Southwest, Wyoming, and Nebraska, renewing her friendship with Annie Sadilek Pavelka.

1917   Discovers Jaffrey, New Hampshire, as a place to work and escape the city and finishes *My Ántonia* there.

1918   *My Ántonia* published in October.

1920   Begins her association with publisher Alfred A. Knopf, who in September brings out the short story collection *Youth and the Bright Medusa,* which includes stories from *The Troll Garden* and "Coming, Aphrodite!."

1922   Lectures at Breadloaf School, Middlebury, Vermont, in July. Visits Grand Manan Island in August, where she will eventually build a vacation cottage with Edith Lewis. *One of Ours* is published by Knopf in September. On December 27 Cather is confirmed with her parents in the Episcopal Church.

1923   Awarded Pulitzer Prize for *One of Ours* in May. *A Lost Lady* published in September.

1925   After visiting Tony and Mabel Dodge Luhan and D.H. Lawrence in Taos, New Mexico, Cather discovers in Santa Fe Rev. William Howlett's biography of Father Joseph Machebeuf, a major source for *Death Comes for the Archbishop. The Professor's House* published in September, the middle section, "Tom Outland's Story," based on Cather's 1915 visit to Mesa Verde.

1926   Summers in New Mexico. *My Mortal Enemy* is published in October.

1927   *Death Comes for the Archbishop* published in September.

1928   Charles Cather dies in March. Willa makes her first trip to Quebec in June and begins writing *Shadows on the Rock.* In December her mother suffers a stroke in California.

1929   Spends spring in Long Beach, California, to be near her mother.

1930   Awarded the Howells medal of the American Academy of Arts and Letters for *Death Comes for the Archbishop.*

1931   *Shadows on the Rock* published in August. One month later Mary Virginia Boak Cather dies in California. During the holiday season Willa visits Red Cloud for the last time.

1932   In August *Obscure Destinies* published, a collection of three short stories, including "Neighbour Rosicky," a story based on the Pavelka family.

1933   Awarded Prix Femina Americain for *Shadows on the Rock.*

1935   *Lucy Gayheart* published in February.

1936   During the spring begins revising her work for Houghton Mifflin's Library Edition. Essay collection *Not Under Forty* published by Knopf in November.

1938   Visits Virginia birthplace in April for the first time in twenty-five years to collect material for *Sapphira and the Slave Girl.* Isabelle McClung dies in October.

1940   In December *Sapphira and the Slave Girl* published.

1944   Receives the National Institute of Arts and Letters Gold Medal for fiction in May.

1945   Completes her last story, "The Best Years."

1947   24 April, dies of a massive cerebral hemorrhage in her New York apartment. Burial is three days later in Jaffrey Center, New Hampshire.

1

Historical Context

Willa Cather was born in depressed, post–Civil War Virginia, from which her extended family began to emigrate by degrees to take advantage of land opportunities in the West. When she arrived in Nebraska at the age of nine, Cather was shocked by its bleakness but forced to discover its unique beauty and participate in life on a somewhat primitive level. This uprooting, more cultural than geographical, proved formative for her career as a novelist, giving her the opportunity to observe pioneer country-making from the perspective of an older culture. Cather experienced a more diverse population in Nebraska than she would have in Virginia, for the prairie farms and town of Red Cloud were a melting pot of New Englanders, Southerners, Scandinavians, Germans, Slavs, and French Canadians. Although she later blamed her fellow Nebraskans for deficiency of vision in devoting themselves to security and creature comforts, she herself benefited from the jingoistic energy that propelled William Jennings Bryan into national politics and from living where, for however brief a period, it was exciting to hear operatic arias played on an upright in a prairie town, to discover the Virgilian dimension of the westward march of civilization, and to believe that a new integrating culture would develop into a golden age as heroic as the image of the plow against the sun at the end of the second book of *My Ántonia*. This, indeed, was her initial hope and her sustaining material, her palette of rich colors, the chiaroscuro she would achieve through the blending of national and racial heritages, folkways, and artistic traditions.

The urban East that Cather experienced as a professional young woman, first in Pittsburgh and finally in New York, was, in its own way, as exciting and diverse. Provincial cities were becoming world metropolises. The new rich were sacking Europe for art treasures and purchasing titles there, and exploiting the immigrants coming in waves to America's shores, but also organizing museums and symphony orchestras and building opera houses. Magazines and newspapers were multiplying to satisfy a varied and growing population's craving for diversion and information, and Cather was able to participate in this new industry, eventually at its muckraking climax in New York as managing editor of *McClure's Magazine*. During her long preparation for the novel writing she was to begin in her late thirties, magazine affiliations kept her in touch with the performing and visual arts as well as literature. (Her turn-of-the-century reviews of plays, concerts, exhibits and fiction fill three substantial volumes.) This exposure plus the contacts with leading writers of the day occasioned by her position at *McClure's* would give her mature fiction surprisingly accomplished aesthetic dimensions and enable her to develop subtexts through a rich variety of allusions. Cather as a novelist and America matured together, for the novel was becoming the national art form. Like some fashionable contemporaries, she considered herself a Jamesian and claimed that Henry James was the greatest mind dedicated to fiction. Like others of her upstart generation—Frank Norris, Stephen Crane, and Jack London—she blamed William Dean Howells for being too tame, although he continually encouraged writers to do what her friend and local colorist Sarah Orne Jewett inspired her to do, to write honestly about the places and the people one knew well, to share with others the feelings and aspirations involved in growing up in offbeat places, to help people know each other better, to develop in oneself and encourage in others what Cather herself would later call the gift of sympathy for one's own fictional world and the worlds of others.

Europe was the likely destination of the girl who read the classics in Red Cloud, rhapsodized over English poetry and French novels and plays as a university student in Lincoln, and found old foreign-born housekeepers on the prairie stimulating company. 1902 was a landmark year for Cather, for it introduced her firsthand to the cultures she inherited as an American. Unlike certain other American writers she admired, such as Henry James and Edith Wharton, however, Cather was decidedly nativist, owing to her Nebraska childhood and adolescence, and Europe was only an extension of her fictional world, never its essence. Thus 1912 was as important a year for her, when she visited the ruins of the Anasazi cliff dwellers in the Southwest. Like Europe, the Southwest brought her back and back again. This region made her rethink Nebraska, see it against a perspective of native as well as immigrant cultures.

She was forty when she published her first Nebraska novel, *O Pioneers!*, having learned to rely on memories of her introduction to Nebraska as her primary source—experiences now colored by reading, listening to music, and appreciating paintings during her magazine years. The results are her best novels, in which the materials of realism are filtered through the glow of cultivated consciousness, just as her landscapes radiate with the light of the setting sun. The "romantic" subjects of her naturalist contemporaries—grotesques, violence, sexual disorders—are distanced in her novels through remembering sensibilities, whether Jim Burden's in *My Ántonia*, Niel Herbert's in *A Lost Lady*, Godfrey St. Peter's in *The Professor's House*, or Jean Marie Latour's in *Death Comes for the Archbishop*. When one penetrates the glow, however, Cather's material is not as wholesome or positive as it at first seems. The abnormalities, frequently the result of characters being raised in bleak and empty places, are then detectable—confused sexual orientation, self-pity, and unhealthy escapism. Cather, then, through a unique combination of influences and experiences, was able to combine the Jamesian novel with the naturalistic, to blend cultivated sensibilities with sensational subjects.

In each book she experimented in her own quiet way, always informed by her lifelong interest in art and music techniques. In her first novel, *Alexander's Bridge,* she applied Jamesian touches to the tragedy of an ambitious architect, a Westerner like herself. *The Song of the Lark,* autobiographical but less filtered through memory and more Dreiserian than *O Pioneers!,* tells the story of a working-girl artist who resembles Dreiser's Carrie Meeber socially and James's Isabel Archer in intelligence and will. In *My Ántonia* Cather experimented with point of view by having the memory of her narrator design as well as reflect the prairie materials she had tapped in *O Pioneers!.* The Great War, fought during the genesis and writing of *My Ántonia,* wrenched her from this remembered past and motivated her first and last frontal attack on contemporary America in *One of Ours.* Awarded the 1922 Pulitzer Prize, this story of a Nebraska soldier who dies in France believing the United States better than it is and France better than any country can be resembles Sinclair Lewis's satirical realism in expressing Francophile Cather's disappointment with America's materialistic values. Having developed late as a novelist and therefore being older than most of her literary contemporaries, she found herself out of step with Fitzgerald's Jazz Age and retreated into the past in *A Lost Lady,* allowing memory and consciousness to distance the action and contribute significance to the classic story of a fallen woman in a pioneer town. By the time she wrote *The Professor's House,* in which the discovery of Mesa Verde is inserted into the story of a disillusioned history teacher in much the same way as the lovers' tragedy is inserted into Alexandra's story in *O Pioneers!,* Cather had fully developed the intellectual filtering consciousness that became a refuge where she could work out her problems during increasingly trying postwar times. The spiritual drama *My Mortal Enemy,* in contrast, is experimental in its objectivity—the antithesis of the cluttered Dreiserian novel—a reaction to modern materialism using a somewhat depersonalized narrator to reduce the novel to its bare bones. *Death Comes for the Archbishop* and *Shadows on the Rock* are unique as historical novels alternating between legends and tales of adventure and the reflective moods of memory-laden protagonist filters. In these novels Cather replaced her prairie farmers with pioneer missionaries and her Nebraska past with North America's Spanish and French heritages, creating worlds of escape in which to examine the universal need for order and meaning. Her final Nebraska novel, *Lucy Gay-heart*, seems an insipid romance until it reverses itself in the last section and becomes a drama of reconciliation for the man who rejected the heroine. Cather used her Virginia beginnings as the setting of her final novel, *Sapphira and the Slave Girl*, in the last section of which she herself appears as narrator, thus linking the ante-bellum South and the World War II era. This story of evil and slavery, deliverance and freedom, like *Archbishop* and *Shadows*, addresses the contemporary world obliquely but perceptively.

Cather lived from the last days of pioneering in the West through two world wars and into the atomic age—a course of history confirming her belief that her country and the world had lapsed spiritually. But she kept writing, although retreating further into the past, about the simple joys and sorrows of family life, and growing more interested in people than in the art of fiction—her last completed story, "The Best Years," implies much about the essential benignity of her last years. Her quest had taken her from Nebraska to the East, returned her to Nebraska, led her to the Southwest, to Quebec, and then to Virginia. Her fiction is being read and studied today more than ever, as she takes her place beside Faulkner as one who mythologized her province and linked it to the world. "We have nothing better than she is," poet Wallace Stevens once wrote to a friend. "She takes so much pain to conceal her sophistication that it is easy to miss her quality."

2

The Importance of the Work

Apparent simplicity, actual complexity is perhaps Cather's most significant achievement in *My Ántonia*. It is one of two novels that establish her as a major American novelist of the twentieth century. The other, *Death Comes for the Archbishop* (the saga of Catholic missionaries in nineteenth-century New Mexico), although a more consistently artistic achievement, has less immediate appeal and is more removed from the events of the novelist's life. Perhaps because *My Ántonia* is so close to Cather's own experiences, there are intriguing problems beneath its controlled surface and transparent prose. These include the adverse effects of cultural deprivation, social prejudice, sexual confusion, midlife and marital crises, and lapses in community values. The story of children discovering the beauties and terrors of a vast new country and of themselves is the essence of the novel's popularity. And its availability to us, the communication of this surface story in a style that seldom calls attention to itself, enhances this popularity. When the novel develops into purple rhapsodies expressive, it can be argued, of narrator Jim Burden's difficulties and sentimentality rather than Cather's, the style does call attention to itself and we can glimpse below the surface. The dichotomy between Cather and Jim Burden is the crack in the apparently wholesome, upbeat surface.

In essence, the novel is the memoir of a middle-aged lawyer whose failed marriage leaves him unloved and alone and whose childhood in Nebraska at the end of the pioneer period becomes in retrospect the happiest time of his life, the period of potential and expectancy before the disappointments of adulthood. Also, the world at war (the novel was begun in 1916) accompanies Jim Burden's malaise and, in effect, his situation is the situation of the nation: there is an obvious need for sanctuary, for the connection to meaning provided by the woman Jim's pioneer childhood enshrines. This figure, virtually an icon, provides Jim with a set of valuable opposites: Ántonia (the minority culture) is female, foreign-born, poor, agricultural, fruitful, and Catholic; Jim Burden (the dominant culture) is male, American-born, privileged, urban, childless, and Protestant. There are shades of *Huckleberry Finn* in this, in the celebration of close-to-nature childhood before life's complexities limit freedom and ruin potential, and in the celebration of cultural opposites, in Twain's case Jim, from whom narrator and reader draw strength and meaning. In both novels the values of the dominant culture become suspect.

Cather's novel offers childhood and the comfortable matriarch, both of which satisfy universal yearnings. These she enhances through echoes of ancient literatures. The drama of nature's seasons in Nebraska echoes Virgil's celebration of pastoral life in the *Georgics*; the story of the girl whose greatness lies in surrendering to inevitability recalls the Mary of Matthew and Luke, and the scene in Ántonia's orchard has its genesis in the Homeric "Hymn to Demeter." Yet *My Ántonia* fits securely into the literary context of its time. As postrealism, it moves from a detailed presentation of certain times and places to romantic idealism as a way to survive the disillusionments of the Fitzgerald and Hemingway era. It accomplishes these things in an intentionally nonformulaic manner. "*My Ántonia* . . . is just the other side of the rug, the pattern that is supposed not to count in a story," Cather said. "In it there is no love affair, no courtship, no marriage, no broken heart, no struggle for success. I knew I'd ruin my material if I put it in the usual fictional pattern. I just used it the way I thought absolutely true." What is missing and why it is missing will continue to tease readers for a long time and may imply much about American life in the twentieth century.

3

Critical Reception

Cather's biographer, James Woodress, notes the appeal of *My Án-tonia* to both the college freshman interested in the simple, human story of people facing recognizable problems and the university professor who finds in it "a richness of allusion, myth, and symbol presented by one of the great stylists of this century." When Cather's publisher sent a copy to Justice Oliver Wendell Holmes, Jr., in 1930, the eighty-nine-year-old jurist responded that the book "lifts me to all my superlatives. . . . It has unfailing charm, perhaps not to be defined; a beautiful tenderness, a vivifying imagination that transforms but does not distort or exaggerate—order, proportion." Such a glowing tribute obscures the fact that *My Ántonia* grew out of a complex personal crisis in Cather's life. In the winter of 1916 Isabelle McClung, to whom Cather had been deeply attached for many years, announced her engagement to a concert violinist; she also decided to sell the McClung family home in Pittsburgh, thus depriving Cather of a congenial refuge from New York as well as of emotional intimacy. Cather took comfort in a visit to New Mexico the following summer, return-

Major studies cited in this chapter are listed in the Bibliography.

ing to Nebraska in August for a stay of several months. Sometime during this period she visited the farm of her old Bohemian friend Annie Sadilek, now married and the mother of many children. There was obvious contentment in this visit and, by the time Cather returned to New York, inspiration for her new novel. Annie became the focus of the memories of a first-person narrator who, although male, resembled Cather in being uprooted from Virginia and transported to the bleak Nebraska prairie at an early age. The result, *My Ántonia* (1918), so uplifting, charming, and indefinable to Justice Holmes and generations of readers, is no longer considered quite so optimistic or even wholesome. Always popular with the general reader, it has only recently become a classic in the academic sense, generating scores of conflicting, analytical articles and literary debates.

Reception and Early Estimates

As Cather's fourth novel, and her third to be set in the West, *My Ántonia* drew attention as the work of an established writer. H. L. Mencken enthusiastically touched most bases in commending Cather's style as "having lost self-consciousness," her "feeling for form" as having "become instinctive," and her "grip upon her materials" as "extraordinary." "I know of no novel that makes the remote folk of the western prairies more real than *My Ántonia*," he wrote, "and I know of none that makes them seem better worth knowing." Mastery of the Nebraska setting also impressed reviewers in the *New York Times* and *New York Sun*, the latter noting the unconventional storytelling and the importance of Jim Burden as narrator. The nucleus of later confusion over who is the protagonist can be detected in early reviews. The *Nation* critic declared the novel the "portrait of a woman," as did Henry W. Boynton in *Bookman;* however, *New York Call Magazine*'s reviewer appreciated Ántonia as unconventional and stirring but thought her no more important than the physical background of the story. N. P. Dawson saw the work as effectively combining realism and naturalism, and he noted the structural principle of stories within stories, "all as neatly unfolding as a set of Chinese boxes." Perhaps the best all-around contemporary estimate of *My Ántonia* is Randolph Bourne's, who recognized in it the realist's command of material, knowledge of the countryside, and understanding of its people. He praised the "gold charm" of its style for enriching the subject and also its uncluttered design, which distinguished it from much contemporary realism: "It has all the artistic simplicity of material that has been patiently shaped until everything irrelevant has been scraped away." The unconventionality of the narrative is only apparently artless, he realized: "No spontaneous narrative could possibly have the clean pertinence and grace which this story has." He defined Jim's vision as "romantic" and Ántonia as the "imaginative center" of *his* memoir. With this book, he claimed, Cather "has taken herself out of the rank of provincial writers" and given us a modern, universal interpretation of the spirit of youth.

The feeling that Cather had arrived with *My Ántonia* was shared by Carl Van Doren, who three years after the novel came out distinguished her work from that of local colorist Sarah Orne Jewett, whose *The Country of the Pointed Firs* had been a major influence on her. He credited Cather with depicting rather than, like Jewett, merely echoing heroic activities but recognized that her full-bodied, Whitmanesque feeling for life had been disciplined by Jewett's taste and intelligence. However, troubled by the novel's structural irregularities, like the "largely superfluous" introduction, he admonished her "to find the precise form for the representation of a memorable character," that it is not enough merely to free oneself "from the bondage of 'plot.'" Cather's connection to the local color school also occupied T. K. Whipple, who in 1928 saw *My Ántonia* as an improvement over Cather's earlier novels in that most irrelevancies in the interest of setting were subsumed in the portrait of the heroine, and he compared Cather to Hardy in making setting epic in scope and integral to story. In 1933 Marxist critic Granville Hicks, who condemned Cather for turning to a remote world in *Death Comes for the Archbishop*, praised *My Ántonia* as a "faithful re-creation" of the "bleakness and cruelty" of prairie monotony and small-town narrowness. Alfred Kazin was perceptive enough in 1942 to see that Cather could "secede with dignity" from modern America by using nostalgia to create values. He saw the world of *My Ántonia* and the earlier prairie novels as "unique in its serenity. Its secret was the individual discovery, the joy of fulfilling oneself in the satisfaction of an appointed destiny." Maxwell Geismar, a forerunner in the explosion of criticism after Cather's death in 1947, narrowed his focus to specific textual problems, detecting a split between the "ostensible heroine," Ántonia, and Lena Lingard, "who almost runs away with the show." He pointed out that Jim is guilty of the social snobbery he condemns in the young men of Black Hawk, and speculated that Ántonia's rustic qualities in the last book might be the result of Jim's twenty years of "continental sophistication"— "as though she had reverted in some degree to the line of her peasant ancestors while [he] has moved closer to his own more or less aristocratic forebears."

Questions of Structure and Protagonist

The structure of *My Ántonia* became a difficulty for those who saw Ántonia as the main character. British critic David Daiches in his 1951 book-length study of Cather is typical in this regard, faulting her for occasionally losing sight of her theme, which he conceives to be the "development and self-discovery of the heroine." E. K. Brown and Leon Edel's 1952 critical biography defends the novel against the charge of being episodic by declaring the various incidents as illuminating one another and contributing to the general tone, but these critics' failure to be specific amounts to a weak defense. The problem they highlight is the male viewpoint, that Cather's strategy of having a narrator fascinated like a man with Ántonia but remaining detached results in emptiness at the novel's center. However, they note the importance of the narrator, that the novel is a record of his impressions as well as of facts and is permeated with a mournful feeling. This emphasis on feeling occupies Richard Giannone, whose 1968 study claims that Ántonia's joie de vivre cannot be conveyed in words, that it is "more a rhythm than a reason" and expressed through music. Giannone puts the d'Arnault episode at the "pulsating center," prepared for by musical references in the first book and then in the scenes at the Harlings', and followed by the "infamous" dances and the playing of old Shimerda's violin at the end. Philip Gerber does little with Jim's role in the 1975 Twayne study. Although Jim's marriage is seen as the reason for his nostalgia and the widely scattered structure the result of his impressions, Jim is labeled "relatively detached" and considered a foil for protagonist Ántonia.

The most comprehensive handling of structure is James E. Miller's 1958 essay, which explores the "emotional unity," the reader's "aroused feeling," as produced and controlled by Jim's sensibility. The novel is not about a real Ántonia but about a "personal and poignant symbol . . . of the undeviating cyclic nature of all life," a reminder of the "tragic nature of time to bring life to fruition through hardship and struggle only to precipitate the decline and, ultimately, death, but not without first making significant provision for new life to follow, flower and fall." Miller sees the various books as illustrating overlapping cycles of nature's seasons, phases of human life, and stages of civilization, concluding that "*My Ántonia* is . . . ultimately about time, about the inexorable movement of future into present, of present into past." Declaring the story "as much Jim's as it is Ántonia's," Dorothy van Ghent in her 1964 Minnesota Pamphlet takes up the time theme in conceiving the novel as an architecture of images. The plow before the sun becomes "a secret life-symbol" on temple or tomb; homely American details compose into friezelike entablatures and engravings on a pillar; and the hired girls become caryatids. Van Ghent sees images of change and loss in time against the timelessness of images as itself.

John Randall claimed in 1960 that Cather balances two protagonists and that Jim is more important than criticism had indicated up to that time. He sees the novel as a system of contrasts: head (Jim) and heart (Ántonia), past (Jim) and future (Ántonia), contemplative life (Jim) and active life (Ántonia), town life (Jim) and country life (Ántonia); also, there are life and death, warmth and cold, and order and chaos contrasts. Randall is perceptive in noting Jim's significant crisis in moving from his original family in Virginia to his second one in Nebraska, and that Ántonia resembles Hawthorne's Hester Prynne in gaining strength from suffering and being accepted by the community. In 1965 novelist Wallace Stegner, like Randall, balanced Jim and Ántonia while exploring the theme of exiles struggling to find a place between old and new worlds. These worlds meet for Ántonia in nature and nurturing, whereas Jim's burden is to remake civilization in a new place. Like Cather herself, he is lured away and divided against himself by education but reunited with his heart in returning to Nebraska and Ántonia. In an important 1969 analysis Terence Martin views the novel in terms of Jim's conflicting impulses toward Lena and Ántonia, between forgetfulness and remembering. He sees Jim as defining both theme and structure, and the novel as presenting his story, not Ántonia's; it is drama of memory, of "how he has come to see Ántonia as the epitome of all he has valued." Virgil's line about the "best days" applies to Ántonia and to the past, where meaning resides for an unhappy man.

Refocusing the novel from Ántonia's development and self-discovery to Jim's, then, addresses many of the complaints about unrelated incidents and about Ántonia's occasional departure from center stage.

Classical Backgrounds

The classics of Greek and Rome are organically pervasive in Cather's fiction and provide as well a rich source of allusions argued L. V. Jacks in 1961. Cather not only evokes Virgil's poetry in My Ántonia, but she was preoccupied with Virgil himself and perhaps identified with him. Six years earlier, Curtis Dahl evaluated Cather's understanding of the themes she incorporated from Virgil's Georgics: celebration of patria, pastoral life, and childhood. Dahl concluded that Cather gave a nineteenth-century American interpretation to Virgilian themes, that Virgil did not prefer pastoral to heroic poetry or childhood to adult life, was not establishing a tradition but following prescription when invoking the muse, preferred philosophy to farming, and wrote a national rather than local poem.

The definitive treatment of *My Ántonia* and the pastoral tradition is in David Stouck's 1975 book-length study of Cather. He sees the pastoral mode as key to understanding Jim's poignant compulsion to return to the past, for implicit in the pastoral art is both the desire to return and the futility of such a return. The novel's tension is between Jim's attempt to cheat time, "to shape a happy and secure world out of the past," and the chronological form of his memories. The pastoral dream is most clearly realized in the "sense of timelessness and spacelessness" of the first book in which disturbing realities are transformed by nostalgia into beautiful memories, but in the second book both time and space restrictions (sex and urban life) challenge the pastoral world. The third book introduces the "imaginative process whereby [Jim's] past experiences are translated into aesthetic forms"; in the last book, although there are reminders of change, sex has been eliminated, and Ántonia and her house relate to Grandmother Burden and hers, thus returning Jim to the beginning. Three years after Stouck's book, Richard Harris narrowed the focus of the pastoral tradition in Cather by applying elements of the Renaissance pastoral to *My Ántonia:* simplicity and beauty of location, erotic idealism, harmony between humanity and nature, and evidence of regenerative powers in nature and its goddess.

The epic rather than pastoral tradition provides Paul A. Olson with an approach to Cather's novel in his 1981 redefinition and application of the epic to American literature of the plains. He makes Ántonia the heroic creator of the new civilization and Jim the hymner singing her accomplishments. In "a nuance here and there" Cather suggests the Homeric sea in the red grass, the suicide of Dido in old Shimerda's, the Cyclops' hunger in the story of the wolves, Pluto's rape of Proserpina in the Wick Cutter episode, the Elysian fields in the fields where the plow is magnified, and so on. Cather's unique achievement is a "georgic epic," a celebration of the snake-ridden garden as the best of the new civilization. Four years earlier, Evelyn Helmick "Nebraskaized" the classic myths by carefully illustrating how Cather re-creates the ancient Eleusinian ritual in the last book of her novel, where Jim experiences epiphany and spiritual transformation through initiation into matriarchal mysteries of the earth. Helmick sees Ántonia as Persephone emerging from the earth after the necessary human sacrifice, the d'Arnault episode as a Dionysian "rhapsody to man's instinctive urge to pleasure," Lena as a fertility goddess, and so on.

The classical dimension of Cather's fiction is a fruitful one in need of further exploration, and an important one because it illuminates the universal significance she saw in her frontier material.

OTHER TRADITIONS

Ongoing attempts to place *My Ántonia* in the realistic tradition are to be expected, considering its native setting, the reason Cather wrote the novel, and her eschewing of the conventional plot. Warner Berthoff, in 1965, saw the novel as the apex of Cather's portrayal of the actual social history of a region, and nine years earlier Howard Mumford Jones credited her with capturing an authentic moment in the development of America. John J. Murphy's 1984 analysis of Cather's filtering through the Jamesian sensibility of Jim Burden the violent material and abnormalities favored by contemporaries like Crane, Norris, London and Dreiser credits Cather with combining both realistic and naturalistic traditions. The American West angle concerns Murphy in a 1982 comparison of Cather's novel and Owen Wister's *The Virginian*. After detailing the careers of Ántonia, Wister's Jeff, and the two narrators, Jim and the tenderfoot, Murphy defines the West of each novel according to what its hero represents: Wister's symbolizes the establishment West of WASP Americans, but Ántonia represents "a counter culture in the West, a backward life rather than progress." In 1978 Randall L. Popken attempted a similar comparison using Hamlin Garland's *Boy Life on the Prairie,* concluding that where Cather allows Jim to escape into memory from malignant forces, Garland refuses to provide Lincoln Stewart with such false optimism. William Stuckey took Cather to task for comparable reasons in 1972, preferring *The*

Great Gatsby to *My Ántonia* because, unlike Cather, who combines realistic skepticism and romantic vision in Jim, Fitzgerald divides Jay Gatsby's romantic re-creation of Daisy Buchanan from realist Nick Carraway's communication of it to the reader: "Jim's problem (which is also Miss Cather's)," argues Stuckey, "is that he cannot get Ántonia into romantic focus until he is far enough away to keep from seeing the things that make her seem unromantic." This failure, he concludes, is one of sensibility as well as technique, "the imposing of . . . strong and intensely personal feelings upon a sometimes intractable world."

Robert E. Scholes turns to an earlier American tradition in his 1962 application of R. W. B. Lewis's American Adam myth to Cather's novel. Both Jim and Ántonia are innocents in the garden, but he distinguishes between them because Jim's background is WASP and hers is Bohemian Catholic. Jim's fall, unlike her traditional sexual one, is a complex failure of happiness, and only through her—through the life of her children—can he have a future. A year earlier, Edwin T. Bowden contrasted Cather's novel with *The Deerslayer* and *Huckleberry Finn* as a study of frontier isolation based, unlike Cooper's novel, on real frontier experiences and, unlike Twain's, on adult responses to isolation. In Cather's "raw middle frontier" the family unit is a defense against isolation, and Ántonia's achievement involves mixing family and prairie, connecting to "something complete and great," and making a country out of the raw materials the frontier offers.

The British romantic poets provided Susan J. Rosowski with an approach to the novel in her 1986 book-length study of Cather. She sees *My Ántonia* as defying analysis, as "a continuously changing work" in the Wordsworthian tradition, a successful balancing of the world of ideas and the world of experience through imaginative fusion. In this interpretation Jim becomes a reacting mind, Ántonia is the object, and tension exists in the mind's attempt to control intractable experience according to sexist and other preconceptions. Tension is also evident in the beauty and fear fostered by nature and between childhood's sense of timelessness and the changes evident during adolescence and adulthood, although these are subsumed in Ántonia as "mediator between man and nature." Earlier, in 1978, Evelyn H. Haller had reached back to Chaucer's Parson's Tale to demonstrate the novel's emblematic portraits of the Seven Deadly Sins and emphasize moral vision. Ántonia herself becomes Charity, the greatest virtue, for even her faults had resulted from abundance of love.

DARK UNDERCURRENTS

The tendency among recent critics of My Ántonia is to dislodge it from its nitch as a work of country-life optimism by exploring undercurrents of death, violence, and sex. In 1967, Isabel Charles linked Jim to Mr. Shimerda as a Thanatos (Death) character, arguing that they provide a dark frame for the vibrant story of Ántonia's Eros (Love) nature. Self-defeated like the old man, Jim is ordained by him in a sacramental laying on of hands to nurture and protect his valuable daughter, but he fails to see this through. Three years later Lois Feger listed several factors in her attempt to establish the dark dimension, seeing futility in the Virgilian epigraph "*Optima dies . . . prima fugit*" ("The best days are the first to flee") and in Jim's life. The novel is replete with images of death and cold; ugliness is associated with reality and beauty with lies in the winter description of Black Hawk; the dark cloud moving westward during the summer storm in book 1 foretells doom; even the heroic plow in the circle of the sun ends in diminishment. Additionally, Jim is savagely cruel to Ántonia after the Cutter episode, and his failure to cross class lines with either Lena or Ántonia make his condemnation of the town self-mockery. The episodes, inserted stories, and anecdotes (Peter and Pavel's tale of wolves, the tramp suicide, the account of Ántonia's ruin), unrelated and functionless for many critics, have unhappiness as a common theme.

In 1971 Blanche Gelfant examined the sexual theme at the heart of My Ántonia and changed the course of criticism on the novel. First of all, she challenged the critical views that made the novel into a glorious celebration of life, a defective work of art, or the product of a reliable narrator. She claimed that Jim belongs to "a remarkable gallery of characters for whom Cather invalidates sex," who invest their energies elsewhere and see sex as destructive and connected to death. Jim reshapes his past to purify it, make it a safe refuge from sex and disorder, and in the process flees from historical truth. He cannot see (nor can Cather, Gelfant insists) that our present disorder stems from this past; he is a romantic, a mythmaker who falsifies the past into "an affecting creation story, with Ántonia [denuded of sensual appeal] a central fertility figure." Book 3 represents Jim at the crossroads between Lena or full sexuality and Ántonia or a return to childhood; however, in his memory of Lena, sex is purified through art, and during the performance of *Camille* art replaces life. The snake episode represents Jim's burrowing into his unconscious; the wolves story amounts to rejection of the bride; Ántonia's ruin confirms the dangers of sex, and so on.

In 1982 Loretta Wasserman challenged Gelfant and earlier critics who claimed that Cather was incapable of writing convincingly about heterosexual relationships or that normal sex is barred from her fictional world. Cather, in fact, acknowledged erotic experiences as contributing to the life of the artist and made Jim's Lincoln encounter with Lena beneficial to both of them. Although their affair is convincingly suggestive, it is not marked by passion; they are not like the lovers in *Camille*, which becomes, then, a "window to another world." In the same year as Wasserman's article, David Stouck tried to bring sanity to the growing interest in Cather's sexual preference and its implications in her fiction. He provides background on Cather's special friendship with Pittsburgh socialite Isabelle McClung and the crisis she experienced when Isabelle married in 1916. He relates Cather at this juncture to Jim Burden: "In her forties, unmarried, without children, and without the love of Isabelle to give her a sense of purpose, she probably felt like Jim Burden, who is similarly childless and disillusioned, and lives very much to himself." Like Jim, she traveled back to Nebraska to take comfort in old friendships and began a novel that assesses human relationships, both friendship and marriage.

A sensitive handling of Cather's life to explain this novel is neither the intention nor method of Deborah Lambert's 1982 essay. Lambert uses Gelfant's speculations about sex in the novel to conclude that Cather was a lesbian "who could not, or did not, acknowledge her homosexuality and who, in her fiction, transformed her emotional life and experiences into acceptable, heterosexual forms and guises." The guise is, of course, the assuming of a male narrator mask to deny both womanhood and lesbianism, which are discredited and outlawed in a patriarchal society. According to Lambert, Cather was sexually attracted to Annie Sadilek Pavelka, the inspiration for Ántonia, as well as to Isabelle McClung, transposing her feelings for Annie to Jim but restricting eroticism to the point that there is emptiness (as Brown noted earlier) at the heart of the novel. Two years later, and without shrillness, Patrick W. Shaw applied the writings of Sigmund Freud and Norman O. Brown to *My Ántonia* to conclude that through the feminine sensitivity of Jim and the masculinity of Ántonia, Cather represented the two halves of her own psyche and celebrated the guiltless anarchy of pregenital life, when the child experiences a sense of eternity rather than the linear perspective of birth, life, and death. The reason, Shaw explains, for what some see as the novel's emotional emptiness is Cather's refusal to allow intimacy between the two halves of her own nature: "They had to remain pure of each other, else she unconsciously sanctioned the most forbidden of sexual crimes." He sees both characters, more especially Jim, as experiencing submergence before their unique union at the novel's end. For Ántonia this is her thralldom to men; for Jim it is twenty years "cocoon time" (from his departure in darkness at the end of book 4 to his accepting in book 5 the union implied in Ántonia's offering him the silver ring in book 1), during which he becomes aware of his own purpose. This submergence is reflected in the underground sojourns of the badger, prairie dogs, ground owls, and the old rattler, and in Jim's fascination with Mr. Shimerda's grave. Emergence is evident at the end in the explosion of children from the dark cave and into the sun.

Criticism on *My Ántonia* has moved from the general to the specific, from the obvious to the implied, to what the text buries rather than states. Jim definitely has become the target of critical exploration, as has Cather herself, fortunately or not. The conception of this novel during the dark days after Isabelle's marriage fascinates now more than ever, as we come full circle, like Jim, to the beginning.

A READING

4

Raw Materials

James Woodress explains in his biography of Cather how she created fictions about herself, that it is sometimes difficult to tell where reality ends and fiction begins. Much of her published fiction, especially *My Ántonia*, is in this overlapping area. "She turned her own life and experiences into literature to a degree uncommon among writers," claims Woodress. "More than most writers, Cather presents readers with the chance to compare biographical data with its transmutation into art. There is a great deal more factual basis in *My Ántonia* than the bare story outline of the title character and the narrator." Before exploring the text of the novel, we should consider the raw materials from Cather's own life and from the lives of family members and friends that went into its making. My major sources for these materials include, besides the Woodress biography, Mildred Bennett's *The World of Willa Cather* and L. Brent Bohlke's collection of Cather interviews, speeches, and letters, *Willa Cather in Person*.

According to most commentators on her life, Cather suffered a serious shock in 1916, when the woman she loved more than any other person, Isabelle McClung, announced her engagement to marry concert violinist Jan Hambourg. Elizabeth Sergeant, another friend, recalls that when Cather told her of this major change in her personal life, "Her face—I saw how bleak it was, how vacant her eyes. All her natural exuberance had drained away." Not only had Cather lost an intimacy, but the McClung family house in Pittsburgh, where she worked off and on for years under the protection of Isabelle, was put up for sale. Also, the war continued in Europe and endangered, she felt, the values and traditions she held sacred. In the spring of 1916, Cather was fed up with life in New York and escaped to the Southwest, a tonic to her since her first trip to Arizona in 1912. On her way back to Nebraska, she stayed with a brother in Lander, Wyoming, and by the end of August was home in Red Cloud with her family and friends. Some time during this visit, which lasted through November, she visited the Bohemian country and her childhood friend Annie Sadilek, the prototype of Ántonia Shimerda, now married and surrounded by her many children on a comfortable farm. Cather was almost forty-three at this time, a few years younger than her friend, and in a worldly sense very accomplished. She had edited a national magazine, published three novels, collections of stories and poetry, was well traveled, and maintained a fashionable New York apartment where she entertained important people. Like her narrator Jim Burden, she was very successful professionally but less so personally. Like the opera star heroine of her recent novel *The Song of the Lark* (1915), her professional life and personal life were intermeshed, her work had become her personal life: "It's like being woven into a big web," complains Thea Kronborg about her opera career. "You can't pull away, because all your little tendrils are woven into the picture. It takes you up, and uses you, and spins you out; and that is your life." However, the woman who had made it all worthwhile, for whom Cather wrote and to whom she had dedicated two of her books, had left her for another, had left a vacuum unfilled even by bitterness. Bohemian friend Annie had traveled a different route; her achievement was of a different kind and perhaps more solid. Cather's elderly Boston friend Mrs. James T. Fields had quoted Aristotle in her diary that "Virtue is concerned with action; art with production." The challenge for Cather was to bring them together—perhaps Annie Sadilek Pavelka had done that in her life, or together with Willa would represent the fusion. In *My Ántonia* Jim and Ántonia represent the reconciliation of these dichotomies.

Cather gave Jim an altered version of her own story. Like him she had been born in Virginia, Back Creek Valley, outside the town of Winchester, and at the age of nine she was uprooted from this green, hilly, forested world and deposited on the barren prairie of Nebraska. Although she did not experience the heartbreak of losing her parents, she suffered disorientation and felt she could not go on when the family sheep dog given to neighbors broke loose and, dropping her chain, came running across the fields in a futile attempt to join the departing family. Other members of the Cather clan had preceded Willa's father, Charles, and his family to Nebraska. His brother George took his family there in 1873 and was followed four years later by his parents, William and Caroline Cather, who sought a drier climate than Back Creek Valley for their tubercular daughters, one of whom died before they left Virginia, another after arrival in Nebraska, and the third a few years later. Willa's grandparents then had three orphaned children to raise, for two of the daughters had been widows with children. William was a devout Baptist, domineering but patriarchal, a Bible reader who composed beautiful prayers. His wife, Caroline, was a milder, gentler character who wore mourning clothes continually after the death of her last daughter. They are the prototypes of Grandfather and Grandmother Burden in *My Ántonia*. Their house, like the Burdens', was built on two levels, the kitchen entered from a draw. Willa's family lived in this house during their first year in Nebraska.

The Charles Cather party of eleven (parents, four children, mother-in-law, hired girls, etc.) traveled to Nebraska on the Burlington line, arriving at Red Cloud depot on an April day in 1883, and were taken by farm wagons sixteen miles to Catherton, the precinct where George and William had their farms. The ride, unlike Jim Burden's, was in daylight, but Willa's experience, according to a 1913 interview reprinted in Bohlke, was similar to his: "I was sitting on the hay in the bottom of a Studebaker wagon, holding on to the side of the wagon box to steady myself—the roads were mostly faint trails over the bunch grass in those days. The land was open range and there was almost no fencing. As we drove further and further out into the country, I felt a good deal as if we had come to the end of everything—it was a kind of erasure of personality." Thrown upon land "as bare as a piece of sheet iron," Willa said she "had that kind of contraction of the stomach which comes from homesickness." But when she heard her father say "you had to show grit in a new country," she determined, she said in 1921, to have it out with the new country, "and by the end of autumn the shaggy grass country had gripped me with a passion I have never been able to shake. It has been the happiness and curse of my life."

Her foreign playmates in the country were German, not Bohemian. Lydia (Leedy) Lambrecht was Willa's age and explored the country with her, hunting for snakes. Leedy's brother was bitten by a rattlesnake, given whiskey, and taken to a doctor in Red Cloud. Since the snakes that invaded the dugouts or soddies of the early settlers were mostly of the harmless bull variety, they were more of a nuisance than a threat, although occasional rattlers kept women alert, and Grandmother Cather always carried a cane with a steel point and a thong at the top to attach to her waist. One of Cather's interests during that first year was to visit foreign-born families that were homesteading on the prairie and outnumbered the American-born by three to one. "We had very few American neighbors—they were mostly Swedes and Danes, Norwegians and Bohemians," she said in 1913. "I liked them from the first and they made up for what I missed in the country. I particularly liked the old women, they understood my homesickness and were kind to me. . . . These old women on the farms were the first people who ever gave me the feeling of an older world across the sea. Even when they spoke very little English, the old women somehow managed to tell me a great many stories about the old country. . . . I have never found any intellectual excitement any more intense than I used to feel when I spent a morning with one of these old women at her baking or butter making. I used to ride home in the most unreasonable state of excitement." It was with immigrants that Cather celebrated her first Christmas in Nebraska. Woodress cites a 1905 letter describing Christmas festivities at the local Norwegian church, where the Christmas tree was improvised from a box elder wrapped in green tissue paper cut to resemble pine needles.

One of the first stories Cather heard concerning immigrants was the suicide of Frank Sadilek, a Bohemian farmer and the father of the girl who would inspire *My Ántonia*. The details of the suicide and related events, perhaps influenced a bit by Cather's fictionalizing, are available from Annie Sadilek Pavelka herself in a letter she wrote on 24 February 1955, two months before her death at age eighty-six, to Omaha high school student Frances Samland, who had inquired about the details of the suicide. (See Appendix A.) Annie first tells about the family's eleven-day crossing on a ship of Polish immigrants, of their arrival in Nebraska on 5 November 1880, expecting to find a land of milk and honey with beautiful houses and lots of trees—a deceitful picture painted for them by a swindling fellow Bohemian. They were disappointed to discover a barren land of dugouts instead of houses, and wagon tracks instead of roads. Only five acres of their land had been broken from virgin prairie; there was no well on the property, merely a sod shack containing a board bed and a four-lid stove. The first winter was severe and the snow heavy, but they kept warm in their dugout by burning cornstalks, sunflowers, and cow chips. They slept on feather beds and hay mattresses placed on the cold earth. Annie recalls that there was little to eat, no place to go, and nothing to read. These conditions, she says, were hard on her father, who had been a weaver in the old country, a man of high spirits who joked and had many friends. Annie obviously admired him, was often his companion, and describes him as "a man in a milion [*sic*] . . . [who] never swore or used dirty words like other men nor he never drank or play cards [*sic*] he was a clean man in everyway." Then on 15 February 1881 he took his shotgun and said he was going rabbit hunting but failed to return by late afternoon. They found him shot in the head and half sitting behind the board bed in the shack. The body was cold, nearly frozen; the sheriff called it suicide. One of the neighbors made a wooden box for the body, which was buried in a corner of the farm because there were no cemeteries. Annie concludes her letter by telling the student that "most all is true" in the account in *My Ántonia*.

Out of this material Cather created her first published story, "Pe-

27

ter," written when she was a college freshman. (See Appendix B.) This story tells us much about her creative process, what Cather added to the original material and how she reworked it for *My Ántonia*. We recognize in it the fictional prototypes of Mr. Shimerda and Ambrosch. Cather's own culture shock at coming to Nebraska is evident, as is her later fascination with the theater and music. Note that in this early version the old man destroys his fiddle—it is not passed down to his grandson as in the novel. Note too the sometimes self-conscious style; Cather had not yet achieved the effortless unobtrusive style of the novel.

Other influences on the first book of *My Ántonia* include the account of Red Cloud's Dr. Damerell's visit to an English family who placed their annual baby in a hole lined with mattresses in the wall of their dugout, and the story of the wolves told to Charles Cather while Willa was present, also the subject of an 1880s painting by Paul Powis, which hung during Cather's time in the Webster County Court House in Red Cloud and depicts wolves attacking a sledge in a far off European country. The summer storm concluding the first book was probably inspired by one witnessed by Willa, home from college, and her brother Roscoe from their Uncle George's fifty-foot windmill tower. Bennett writes, "The two got so interested in watching the storm come up, with the red harvest moon in the East, the clouds and lightning in the West, and the cattle huddling in the corrals below, that they forgot their own precarious position. . . . Willa had to take off her outer skirts to get down, and . . . blistered her hands clinging to the narrow ladder."

In September 1884 after more than a year on the farm, the Charles Cathers moved to Red Cloud, a town of 2,500 on the Republican River and the Webster County seat, where Charles took up real estate, sold insurance, and arranged loans. Red Cloud in the 1880s was an up-and-coming place. The *Nebraska State Journal* asserted, somewhat unprophetically, that "No town in the state is better off in the line of churches and schools than Red Cloud. . . . Red Cloud is destined to be one of the foremost cities in Nebraska, in time, and in years not distant will be the leading town along the southern border of the state." The Cathers rented a story-and-a-half house too small for their growing family, where Rachel Boak, Willa's maternal grandmother, provided meals for young workmen. The Cathers' neighbors were the Miners, who operated Red Cloud's first department store. The Miner children were Willa's closest Red Cloud friends and appear as the Harling children in *My Ántonia*. Carrie, the eldest, helped her father in the store and is Frances; Mary, the musical one, appears as Julia; Margie, a tomboy, is Sally; Irene, the sensitive one, became Nina; and Hughie Harling appears as Charley, whom Ántonia idolizes in the novel, which is dedicated to Carrie and Irene, "In memory of affections old and true." It was at the Miners' that Willa met Annie Sadilek, their hired girl, whom Willa honored in a 1921 interview with Eleanor Hinman as "One of the people who interested me most as a child. . . . She was one of the truest artists I ever knew in the keenness and sensitiveness of her enjoyment, in her love of people and in her willingness to take pains." Annie's employer, Mrs. Julia Miner, whose piano playing was the first serious music Willa heard, became Mrs. Harling, a clear snapshot of the original, Cather later told her daughter Carrie. Mr. James Miner, the head of the house, appears as the sometimes stern Mr. Harling, who in real life had a scuffle with one of his hired girls for making love on the back porch.

Willa and these Miner children put on circuses in the Miner barn and plays in the parlor. Interest in performers and theater took them to the railroad depot a half dozen times a year to meet the trains bringing stock company players to the Opera House. The children also explored the sandy islands in the Republican River, which Willa christened with names from Robert Louis Stevenson: "Robber's Cave," "Dragon's Slide," "Pirate's Island." They hunted tadpoles and turtles and drowned out gophers. The river area is the locale of Jim's picnic with the hired girls near the end of the second book of the novel, a scene anticipated in Cather's fine 1909 story, "The Enchanted Bluff." Diversion was also provided by traveling Marshall Field salesmen who brought fireworks to town or entertained the population with songs. Another special event was the coming of pianist Blind Boone to the Holland House, formerly the Boys' Home but remodeled and rechris-

Anna Pavelka at age seventeen.
Nebraska State Historical Society

tened by George and Elizabeth Holland, the prototypes of the Gardeners in the novel. Mrs. Holland was a notorious fanatic for cleanliness and notorious too for having jewels that only a privileged few had seen. Boone, rocking back and forth at the keyboard, gave special concerts for their guests. Traveling Italian minstrels would arrive from Colorado in the summers and play for dances held on a platform beneath a bowery of cut willow branches.

Cather's choice of a male narrator for *My Ántonia* is somewhat explained if not justified by the male pose she assumed in Red Cloud and carried into her university years. Her hair was cropped short, initially for easy care when her mother was ill but subsequently as a statement of rebellion. She wore boys' clothes, took boys' parts in theatricals, and was very successful as the merchant father in the 1888 Opera House performance of "Beauty and the Beast." The local paper reported that she "carried it through with such grace and ease that she called forth the admiration of the entire audience." Such nonconformity was a protest against maternal discipline and against the town's narrow-mindedness. Cather objected to the prejudices of the American-born against foreigners. As she stated in a 1923 essay in the *Nation*, "If the daughter of a shiftless West Virginia mountaineer married the nephew of a professor at the University of Upsala, the native family felt disgraced by such an alliance." Also, she lamented the inability of the American-born to have fun. When one of the children was permitted to do a rhythmic dance in a play that Willa and the others were putting on, the mother was ostracized from her church. "At the same time 'moral' enthusiasts were circulating a book entitled 'Ballroom to Hell' which was destined to stamp out the evil of dancing," writes Mildred Bennett in her 1951 study of Cather. "Later Willa said: 'Those who make being good unattractive do more harm than those who strive to make evil attractive.'" The result or cause of Willa's rebel period might have been her intention to be a doctor, which she gave up during her college years. Her adult friends included Doctors G. E. McKeeby and Robert Damerell, and on one of her excursions with Damerell she administered chloroform when a boy's leg had to be amputated. For her high school commencement oration at the Opera

House, her subject was "Superstition *versus* Investigation," a polemic in favor of vivisection and scientific research in general.

Among Red Cloud's notorious citizens was M. R. Bentley, a loan shark who took advantage of immigrant farmers and delighted in being niggardly to his wife. Although Mrs. Bentley gave her husband a start in his business through profits from her millinery shop, he kept her financially dependent by denying her all but the bare essentials of life. "She couldn't have guests because he would complain about expenses," writes Bennett; "and although she wasn't well, she couldn't keep a hired girl because her husband would either get her in trouble or drive her away. Once Mrs. Bentley tried to take painting lessons but hadn't enough money for canvas or brushes." Meanwhile, Bentley, "a fine-looking, dressy man with blonde skin . . . spent generously for himself. . . ." This life of abuse and ill treatment, complicated by the appearance of a girl named Venus, rumored to be Bentley's illegitimate daughter, ended for Mrs. Bentley when her husband shot her and then killed himself. The Bentleys were living in Arkansas at the time of this catastrophe, 10 April 1912. Local newspaper reports correspond to the account of the Cutter murder-suicide in *My Ántonia*, although Bentley did not call in witnesses before he died as Cutter does in the novel. Another community character that must have been of interest to Cather was Fannie Fernleigh, madam of a local house of prostitution. Bennett describes one of her girls, perhaps an inspiration for Lena Lingard, as "a lovely eighteen-year-old blonde who seemed to spend a lot of time buying children's clothes [at Miner Brothers' General Store]. When asked what she did with them, she explained that her little sisters had to be cared for."

Among those who helped prepare Cather for the literary career she would eventually pursue were William Ducker, a well-educated Englishman who took enough interest in the rebel girl to read college Latin with her, and Mr. and Mrs. Charles Wiener, a Jewish couple who spoke German and French, introduced her to French novels, and helped her translate them. Many had contributed to the making of the young woman who, in September 1890, stepped from the train in Lincoln to begin her life at the new University of Nebraska and experience her first taste of urban life. The new prairie city had a population of 35,000 spread out over a wide grid, five hotels, a six-story skyscraper, a telephone company, a waterworks, and shade trees. As a railroad center, Lincoln became a convenient stop for first-rate theatrical and musical companies passing through from Chicago to Denver and the coast. Cather was exposed to artists like Julia Marlowe, Helena Modjeska, the Drews, and Otis Skinner. By 1893 she was reviewing performances for the *Nebraska State Journal.* One of her first reviews was of Clara Morris in *Camille,* which she called "the one great drama of the century." "*Camille* is an awful play," she wrote. "Clara Morris plays only awful plays. Her realism is terrible and relentless. It is her art and mission to see all that is terrible and painful and unexplained in life. It is a dark and gloomy work." "Comments upon the wonderful power of Clara Morris's voice, upon the technical perfection of her acting are utterly unnecessary." Cather's first exposure to grand opera came in her last semester of college when she spent a week in Chicago to hear three operas by Verdi (*Falstaff, Otello,* and *Aida*), Meyerbeer's *Les Huguenots,* and Gounod's *Romeo et Juliette.*

Willa's boyhood phase continued into her Lincoln years. She wore her hair short until her junior year, wore shirts rather than blouses, and specialized in male roles in dramatic productions. Among her friends at this time was Louise Pound, who later became a respected folklorist and the first woman president of the Modern Language Association. Pound, the very feminine product of a sophisticated family, was an accomplished junior when Cather, still a prep at the university, met her. "Cather fell in love, apparently for the first time in her life," writes Woodress. "Whether this love should be considered a serious affair or a short-lived freshman's 'crush' on a senior is arguable. To call this a lesbian relationship, as some critics have done, is to give it undue importance. Pound did not return the affection with anything like the fervor with which it was given. She had many admirers, of both sexes, was not inclined to focus her attention on any one individual, and this relationship came to an abrupt end after about two and a half years." Friendship of a much different kind developed between Cather and English professor Herbert Bates, a native New

Englander who encouraged her literary efforts. Bennett describes him as tall and thin, "ungainly and sarcastic[;] he inspired in his students either great admiration or intense dislike." Of course, Cather admired him and valued her long talks with him. He was an influence on her volume of poetry, *April Twilights* (1903). It was Bates who was so impressed by the story "Peter" that he sent it off to *The Mahogany Tree,* a Boston magazine, where it appeared in May 1892. Bates appears in *My Ántonia* as Gaston Cleric, who helps Jim overcome his infatuation with Lena and continue his studies at Harvard.

To the fledgling author who returned there for holidays and after graduation, Red Cloud and Webster County in general had become Siberia. The young men were rowdy, and social life was less than rustic. She was shocked that during a New Year's dance sandwiches were served from a bushel basket. In her fiction of this period, like "Peter" and "On the Divide" (1896), Nebraska is a forbidding, harsh land unsoftened by the romantic imagination of a Jim Burden. But rescue from Siberia was imminent. In the spring of 1896 Cather was offered the editorship of the *Home Monthly,* a Pittsburgh family magazine with Presbyterian associations, an opportunity that led to drama reviewing for the *Pittsburgh Leader,* other editorial challenges, school teaching, and friendship with Isabelle McClung, whom she met backstage in a theater in the spring of 1899. The socialite daughter of affluent Judge Samuel A. McClung, Isabelle began promoting her new friend's career and invited her in 1901 to live in the McClung home, where a sewing room was converted into a study for her. A year later the two friends traveled through Europe together. In 1906 Cather joined the staff of *McClure's Magazine* and moved to New York. While on assignment in Boston for *McClure's* in 1908, she met distinguished local colorist Sarah Orne Jewett, who told the young writer to use her Nebraska material, to write about what was important to her, and to make it her own by writing the truth.

It is as accurate as it is simple to say that the effect of Jewett's advice combined with Cather's stimulating introduction to the Southwest in 1912 produced *O Pioneers!,* Cather's first Nebraska novel, about which she said, "In this one I hit the home pasture. . . ." Ethel

M. Hockett in a 1915 interview was probably unconscious of the perceptivity of her statement that Cather "went to Arizona for the summer and returned to New York to write *O Pioneers!*." Six years later Cather explained her accomplishment of writing satisfactorily about Nebraska: "It takes a great deal of experience to become natural. People grow in honesty as they grow in anything else. A painter or writer must learn to distinguish what is his *own* from that which he admires. I never abandoned trying to make a compromise between the kind of matter that my experience had given me and the manner of writing which I admired, until I began my second novel, 'O Pioneers!' And from the first chapter, I decided not to 'write' at all—simply to give myself up to the pleasure of recapturing in memory people and places I had believed forgotten. This was what my friend Sarah Orne Jewett had advised me to do. She said to me that if my life had lain in a part of the world that was without a literature, and I couldn't tell about it truthfully in the form I most admired, I'd have to make a kind of writing that would tell it, no matter what I lost in the process." This is what Cather meant when she told Elizabeth Sergeant, "Life began for me when I ceased to admire and began to remember."

She had visited the Bohemian country prior to writing *O Pioneers!* and might have taken up with her old friend Annie Sadilek at that point. Annie was now married to fellow Bohemian immigrant farmer John Pavelka and the mother of many children. (John later appears as the title character in Cather's much-anthologized 1932 story "Neighbour Rosicky," and Annie as his wife, Mary.) She had endured and prevailed over being deserted with child by railroad brakeman James William Murphy. When Cather sought the comfort of the Southwest and Red Cloud friendships in 1916, the year of Isabelle's marriage, Annie became the subject of her art, a salvation figure transformed by the alchemy of memory. *My Ántonia* not only captures Annie with feeling but reveals through Jim Burden the artistic process Cather used to present reality filtered through memory. Although we must distinguish between Jim's romanticizing as the product of a "romantic disposition which often made him seem very funny as a boy" and Cather's "recapturing in memory," the novel is, nevertheless, autobiographical in a double sense. It incorporates the facts of Cather's life while illustrating the way she learned to view, integrate, and write about them. Truly it is a coming home to oneself—for Willa Cather as well as for Jim Burden.

5

The Alembic of Art

My Ántonia is a novel in which vision and arrangement create character. Jim Burden, despite his disclaimer that it "hasn't any form," designs his narrative into patterns that give meaning to his experiences and help him through the crisis years of middle age. Consideration of the memoir he offers us should begin in book 3, "Lena Lingard," which functions as a prism through which this text should be viewed. In it Jim describes his college studies and their setting, "the commodious green-topped table placed directly in front of the west window which looked out over the prairie" (259). Gaston Cleric, his instructor, makes "the drama of antique life" (261) and the great classics, Virgil's *Aeneid* and *Georgics,* and Dante's *Divine Comedy,* live for him. This mental excitement focuses Jim back on his prairie experience rather than on distant worlds: "I suddenly found myself thinking of the places and people of my own infinitesimal past. They stood out

I am indebted in this chapter to Barbara Novak's *American Painting of the Nineteenth Century* (Praeger, 1969), and Michael C. J. Putnam's introduction to his *Virgil's Poem of the Earth* (Princeton University Press, 1979). Cather's views on the Barbizon school and other painters are in *The World and the Parish* and *Willa Cather in Europe.*

strengthened and simplified now . . ." (262). He then quotes from the third book of the *Georgics* to celebrate his boyhood on the prairie, that in the lives of mortals the best days are the first to flee ("*Optima dies . . . prima fugit*"). He ponders Virgil's hope to bring the muse from Greece to bear upon the Latin experience, to "be the first . . . to bring the Muse into my country" (263–64). At this point Jim's childhood friend Lena Lingard re-enters his life, and he applies the great poetry he is studying to her and to the other country girls, Ántonia Shimerda foremost among them, he has left behind on the prairie: "It came over me, as it had never done before, the relation between girls like those and the poetry of Virgil. If there were no girls like them in the world, there would be no poetry" (270). This "revelation" about poetic inspiration, described as "inestimably precious," explains the motivation behind the manuscript Jim presents to Cather's persona a score of years later in the introduction, which distances the memoir from Cather herself. In it, says Cather, "this girl [Ántonia, who] seemed to mean to us the country, the conditions, the whole adventure of our childhood," inspired Jim to write an account of her, "pretty much all that her name recalls to [him]." The account Jim produces is dualistic in nature, involving not only his impressions of this friend but a record of his own somewhat confused passage from boyhood to manhood.

Both aspects are viewed through the arts. Virgil's poem on rustic life in Italy, the *Georgics,* provides Jim with major images, episodes, and themes in his rendition of Ántonia and his country boyhood. The climax of Jim's rite of passage, his affair with Lena Lingard in book 3, involves another important literary work, *La Dame aux Camelias* by Alexandre Dumas, *fils,* a performance of which he attends with Lena before he describes the life they share in Lincoln. Some familiarity with these works and the Bible, an explicit and implicit frame of reference for Jim throughout his memoir, is advisable for an understanding of how he views experience and how Cather sets her novel firmly upon literary traditions. Her significant appreciation and knowledge of painting and, to a lesser degree, music, evident in her reviews during the Lincoln and Pittsburgh years, complement this literature in contributing to Jim's character as he views his past. However, in evaluating the characterization, we should make distinctions between Jim's rendering of events taking place before he became conditioned to viewing them aesthetically—that is, the events of the first two books—and events taking place after he began to view them as set pieces. "Lena Lingard" becomes, then, an interfacial book, and distinguishing between the books on either side of it helps explain the increasing sentimentality and stylistic excesses evident in certain episodes in the last two books.

BIBLICAL BORROWINGS

Jim's use of the Bible to enhance the significance of the raw materials that Cather employs in the novel is evident from the start, in the night ride over the prairie, during which the terrain suggests chaos, land in the process of creation, "not a country at all, but the material out of which countries are made" (7). Humanity's evolving from the earth is depicted in the Shimerda family's emergence from the dugout when the Burdens visit them for the first time, the language lesson that follows recalling Adam's naming of the animals, and the subsequent exploration of the country by Jim and Ántonia, the process of acquaintance with new creation. The search for the Promised Land is echoed in the Mormon sunflower trails, "the sunflower-bordered roads . . . to freedom" (29), and in the description of the prairie sunset as "like the bush that burned with fire and was not consumed" (40). Grandfather Burden, the patriarch, reads from the Bible, first from Psalm 47, which extends Yahweh's kingdom over all nations, and then the first two chapters from Matthew, the account of Christ's birth. When the elder Burdens go to the Shimerdas after the suicide "they looked very biblical as they set off . . ." (100).

There are many less specific biblical borrowings and echoes. Most obvious is Jim's struggle with the snake, "the ancient, eldest Evil" (47), a struggle made clearly sexual in its variation in the second book when he contends with Wick Cutter. The sexual dimension is prepared for early in this book when Jim notes that the state of the happy children in the Harling garden will be changed by puberty. After Mr. Shimerda's death, Anton Jelinek's arguments on the efficacy of the Sacrament recall the words of Christ in John 6:57–58. Mr. Shimerda's stiffened body is juxtaposed with the stiff paper Christ Child Jim hangs on the Christmas tree to remind us of the promise of resurrection, hinted at later in the coming of spring at the end of the first book and the explosion of children from the cave in the last. The Christmas story of Matthew and Luke echoes in Widow Steavens's account of the birth of Ántonia's child; and Jim's subsequent farewell scene with Ántonia, illuminated by the sun and the moon, recalls Revelation 12:1, traditionally applied to the Virgin Mary, and prepares for Ántonia's enthronement in the orchard at the end of the novel, reminiscent of the Coronation of the Virgin depicted in medieval icons and loosely based on the Song of Songs 4:8. Cather's biblical subtext, further developed in my commentary, is an unusual one for an American western in that it incorporates Ántonia's Catholic tradition and Jim's Protestant one to make events notable.

GEORGICS BORROWINGS

Cather invites the reader more emphatically to pursue the *Georgics* connection than the biblical, although the inclusion of Virgil's poem mirrors and adds new dimensions to the Bible by combining classical and Judeo-Christian heritages. The *Georgics* underscores Cather's agricultural theme and calls attention to related others. For example, while georgic 1 resembles the first book of the novel in emphasizing hard work and seasonal changes, it is more than a depiction of rural life. Cultivation of nature in Virgil merely reflects human cultivation, as Michael Putnam notes: "the inner nature of man . . . is as much a challenge to be mastered as the decadent ruggedness of external nature's inborn primitivism. . . . The blight the sky god sends eradicates fields, crops, and beasts. Man's inner weathers destroy himself." The sexual theme developed by Jim provides his second and third books with these human challenges, and the theme of self-discipline is evident in Ántonia's sacrificing of school for field work and later in her recovery from disgrace and dedication to her baby. Georgic 2 depicts the ideal human condition between rustic and urban life, a context of family togetherness and fruitful agriculture, resembling the novel's final book, in which Antonia's family is preserved in an idyllic state, and the end of the first book when Jim seems to hear the corn growing in the night: "under the stars one caught a faint crackling in the dewy, heavy-odoured corn fields where the feathered stalks stood so juicy and green" (137). Georgic 3, from which Cather takes her epigraph, "*Optima dies . . . prima fugit,*" focuses on conflicts caused by sex and death, combining the themes of Cather's first and second books. Virgil sees the sex act and passionate emotions as destructive to humans, reducing them to the level of animals, which is clearly illustrated in Wick Cutter's attempted rape of Ántonia.

Georgic 4 contains a feature characteristic of most Cather novels, an epyllion, defined by L. P. Wilkinson as a "short kind of epic . . . , [a] feature of [which] was that the story had another story inset which is somehow, directly or obliquely, relevant to it, if only by way of contrast." Virgil's epic story is of the agricultural hero Aristaeus, who loses his bees because of his pursuit of Eurydice, killed in flight by a serpent. Aristaeus' passion thus has a blighting effect and causes suffering and death. The inserted story is of Orpheus' lament, his struggles to rescue his wife, Eurydice, from Hades, and owing to his inability to resist beholding her, his final loss of her and his destruction by Thracian women for abjuring sex. Virgil's inclusion of these stories resembles Cather's method of inserting stories throughout her novel—what an early reviewer noted as the structural principle of stories "all as neatly unfolding as a set of Chinese boxes." The wolves episode framed by the story of the Russians and the placing of the Cutter story within the Cuzak story are examples of Cather's use of epyllion-type form.

More significantly, as the musical artist at the heart of Aristaeus' story, Orpheus is the equivalent to Blind d'Arnault, the black pianist who plays at the Boys' Home in "The Hired Girls." Richard Giannone, in analyzing Cather's use of musical representations, sees this episode as the novel's "pulsating center" prepared for by old Shimerda's silent violin and the musicales at the Harlings' and followed by the dances at the Vannis' tent and Firemen's Hall, the *La Traviata* music at the *Camille* performance, and the Cuzak family musicale arranged for Jim. These allusions reflect the interest in and knowledge of music evident in Cather's many reviews of musical performances and the details of vocal training and opera in *The Song of the Lark*, the novel immediately preceding *My Ántonia*. It is fitting, then, that Cather uses a musical figure to communicate Jim's preference for strong emotion and generosity of attitude, Ántonia's instinctively sweet nature, and the general sense of loss that pervades his memoir. The genesis of both d'Arnault's piano playing and Orpheus' song is loss or incompleteness: Orpheus is deprived of Eurydice and d'Arnault of complete manhood. Orpheus' song expresses his own loss as well as Aristaeus' loss of his bees; d'Arnault's playing expresses his own loss as well as Jim's loss of Ántonia. As in Virgil, music has sexual overtones; Putnam speculates that Orpheus' story implies that sexual wildness must be measured but not eliminated. In Cather, d'Arnault's compensation through the piano duplicates Jim's compensation through the memoir for unsatisfactory love relationships.

Other techniques Cather's novel shares with Virgil's poem include the prevalence of set pieces; the paralleling, contrasting, and interweaving of themes; the use of mythology; and kaleidoscopic imagery. Examples of Cather's use of set pieces, or fixed forms set within the text (like Virgil's descriptions of country life, the snake, summer storm, plow, and his use of the epyllion form), include the snake episode, the Russian wolves story, the summer storm at the end of the first book, the plow at sunset during Jim's picnic with the hired girls, and Jim's farewell scene with Ántonia at the end of the fourth book. Cather's themes are arranged, as are Virgil's, in systems of parallels and contrasts. Where Virgil balances the runaway boat with the runaway chariot in georgic 1, Cather balances the Shimerdas' emergence from their dugout with the explosion of Ántonia's children from the fruit cave. Where Virgil balances the havoc caused by sex with that caused by plague in georgic 3, Cather balances the snake episode with the Cutter rape attempt. Contrasts in Virgil between peace and war, and rural and urban life are evident in Cather when the first and fifth books, depicting country life, are compared to the second and third, depicting town and city life; also, contrast is evident between the celebration of Christmas and the suicide of Mr. Shimerda in the barn.

Cather's interweaving of themes is at least apparently Virgilian. Wilkinson cites critics as likening the *Georgics* to a musical composition in many tones "in which a number of themes develop, come to the fore, die away and make place for new ones," which is the method employed by Cather in this novel, as well as in *The Professor's House, Death Comes for the Archbishop,* and *Shadows on the Rock.* Cather indicated that the text of the latter novel was "mainly anacoluthon," which Edward and Lillian Bloom define as evoking "an emotional or moral effect through a temporary suspension of completeness—i.e., like a series of minor suspenses—within the individual actions of the principal framework . . . , the seeming disjunction attained by initiating episodes and then disclosing their resolutions in subsequent appropriate phases of the novel." Where Virgil's theme of death is introduced near the beginning of georgic 3 with the wornout dam, recurs two hundred lines later with the death of Leander, then a hundred lines later with the frozen oxen, and swells to a climax with the plague at the conclusion—Cather's theme of cold and death is introduced in the freezing insect, recurs in the death of Pavel, and climaxes in the suicide of Mr. Shimerda during a blizzard. All these techniques are employed to unify works that (lacking strong narrative lines to hold together set pieces, scenes, episodes, and descriptions) tend to be episodic. Wilkinson sees as analogous to such strategies the arrangement of subjects in wall paintings contemporary to Virgil. Somewhat similar is Judith Fryer's comparison of Cather's method to a series of photographs creating tensions through the spaces between the images rather than through the mystery of destination, the waiting for the end, which is the usual method in a work with strong narrative lines.

Virgil uses myth in the *Georgics* to invest humble things with dignity, to heighten his agricultural material, which is the import of his statement in georgic 3, quoted by Jim in his third book, about bringing the muse from Greece to Italy. The Aristaeus and Orpheus myths function in this way, as do invocations to Pan, the fauns, the country gods, and associations of the spider with Minerva, the stallion with Saturn, etc. In Cather, as Evelyn Helmick points out, Ántonia can be associated with Persephone, her underworld experience being her affair with Larry Donovan and its aftermath, and her seasonal emergence related to her fertility, evident in the figure of the children bursting from the dark cave into the sunlight. Her intimacy with the earth is suggested in the earth tones used to describe her and the statement in the introduction that she "seemed to mean to us the country, the conditions, the whole adventure of our childhood." Jim makes an intriguing comment in this vein when he returns to Ántonia after her disgrace: "I found that I remembered the conformation of the land as one remembers the modelling of human faces" (306). Ántonia's foil, Lena, is obviously Venus-like in her seductive air, her laughter, and her association with water—Colonel Raleigh makes her the gift of a porcelain bathtub; her major complaint about her childhood is that she had to carry water from the windmill on Saturday nights in order to bathe. What is revealing about the Persephone–Venus connection is the quarrel these deities have over Adonis (Jim?), which results in Zeus's decree that the boy spend a third of his time with Persephone, a third with Venus, and a third on his own. Finally, Helmick links the three very sexual Bohemian Marys to the three Maenads, female votaries of Dionysius, and Jim adds a Virgilian touch by expounding on Leo Cuzak's faunlike qualities.

My Ántonia also resembles Virgil's poem in its imagery. What Wilkinson describes as kaleidoscopic imagery in the *Georgics*, directing the inner eye from one range of images to the other—the minute to the far-reaching (the tiny ant pursuing its narrow path and the huge, overarching rainbow)—in an enthusiasm for nature's variety, can be seen in the garden scene at the beginning of "The Shimerdas," where Jim's eye ranges from the limitless fields of shaggy red grass to big yellow pumpkins and then to the minute black spots on the "polished vermillion" backs of the squadrons of little bugs moving around him (p. 18). The same range, but in the opposite direction, is evident later when his eye moves from the tiny freezing insect Ántonia places in her hair to the setting sun transfiguring the "miles of copper-red grass" (40). The pictorial imagery of Virgil's poem includes descriptive detail in the vein of genre and landscape paintings, notes Wilkinson, and the pleasure we can derive from this use of detail is akin to that we derive from such paintings: "The total effect is a panorama of rural life, a supremely artistic documentary." Such pictorial traditions are very evident in Cather's text; and its initial attraction for many readers (including this one) is description. Indeed, the genesis of *My Ántonia* might reside in French painting.

CATHER'S USE OF PAINTING

When Cather visited Barbizon in 1902 there were reminiscences of Nebraska in the primitive huts of mud and stone, the level wheat fields, and the peasant women. What is noteworthy is her association of these women, who anticipate Ántonia, especially as described in the last book of the novel, with the paintings of Jean-François Millet. She noted among the stackers "women bare-headed and brown-faced and broad of shoulders." The gleaners were

> usually women who looked old and battered, who were bent and slow and not good for much else. Such brave old faces as most of these field-working women have, such blithe songs they hum, and such good-humored remarks they bawl at a girl who sees too much of one particular reaper. There is something worth thinking about in these brown, merry old women, who have brought up fourteen children and can outstrip their own sons and grandsons in the harvest field, lay down their rake and write a traveller directions as to how he can reach the next town in a hand as neat as a bookkeeper's. As the sun dropped lower, the merriment ceased, the women were tired and grew to look more and more as Millet painted them, warped and bowed and heavy.

Cather's interest in Millet can be traced back to a comment she made in a review of an exhibit in Lincoln in 1895, when she compared a genre painting by Kentuckian Thomas Noble to Millet's work, say-ing that the Frenchman (unlike the American) "painted for the sake of the people who suffered, never vexing himself about the cause of it." Six years later she again praised the genius of the Barbizon master for making "homely subjects into art." In the same review she singled out a lesser Barbizon painter, Jules Breton, for his "Song of the Lark" (which would provide the title for her third novel), depicting a peasant girl barefoot in a wheat field listening to the bird. In 1913 Millet was again on her mind; in an interview with the *Philadelphia Record*, she described art as a process of simplification:

> Whether it is a pianist, or a singer, or a writer, art ought to sim-plify—that seems to me to be the whole process. Millet did hundreds of sketches of peasants sowing grain, some of them very complicated, but when he came to paint "The Sower," the compo-sition is so simple that it seems inevitable. It was probably the hundred sketches that went before that made the picture what it finally became—a process of simplifying all the time—of sacrificing many things that were in themselves interesting and pleasing, and all the time getting closer to the one thing—It.

Millet certainly contributes to Jim's presentation of Ántonia at various stages in the novel. In his first portrait, her eyes are "big and warm and full of light, like the sun shining on brown pools in the wood. Her skin was brown, too, and in her cheeks she had a glow of rich dark color. Her brown hair was curly and wild-looking" (23). Millet's inspiration is evident later when at sunset Jim watches Án-tonia come up the south draw with her team, "a tall, strong young girl" in her father's boots—"Her outgrown cotton dress switched about her calves, over the boot-tops. She kept her sleeves rolled up all day, and her arms and throat were burned as brown as a sailor's. Her neck came up strongly out of her shoulders, like a bole of a tree out of the turf. One sees that draught-horse neck among the peasant women in all old countries" (122). After she is disgraced and Jim ar-rives to bid her farewell, she stands, again in sunset, leaning on her pitchfork, "thinner . . . and . . . 'worked down,' but there was a new kind of strength in the gravity of her face, and her color still gave her that look of deep-seated health and ardour" (319). Finally, she stands before Jim, "a stalwart, brown woman, flat-chested, her curly brown hair a little grizzled" (331). "She was a battered woman now . . . but she still had that something which fires the imagination, could still stop one's breath for a moment by a look or gesture that somehow revealed the meaning in common things. She had only to stand in the orchard, to put her hand on a little crab tree and look up at the apples, to make you feel the goodness of planting and tending and harvesting at last" (353).

While these portraits definitely reflect Millet and his Barbizon contemporaries, descriptions of people and places elsewhere in the novel reveal the influence of the impressionism that grew out of the Barbizon tradition. Cather's awareness of the American realists and impressionists influenced by these French painters is evident in the 1895 review, when she singles out Frank Benson and Theodore Robinson for praise. She also has good things to say about Winslow Homer's "The Wreck," first prize winner in the Founder's Day competition of the Carnegie Institute Art Galleries in 1897, which she reviewed and was attended by such notables in American painting as William Merritt Chase, John LaFarge, and Frank Duveneck. The connection between this group and Millet is evident when one views a work like Robinson's "The Watering Pots," which uses impressionistic brush strokes and bright colors to depict a Millet-like French peasant woman. Although Homer's realistic paintings of fisherfolk around Tynemouth, England, depict Millet-type substantial females, it is his lighter (in weight and color) American working girl counterparts that seem to influence Jim's picture of Ántonia at the pump in the first book: "we heard the frosty whine of the pump and saw Ántonia, her head tied up and her cotton dress blown about her, throwing all her weight on the pump-handle as it went up and down. She heard our wagon, looked back over her shoulder, and, catching up her pail of water, started at a run for the hole in the bank" (72). Jim's picture of the hired girls in their finery, as on the moonlit night after his commencement, "their white dresses glimmer smaller and smaller down the sidewalk as they went away" (231), and his portraits of Lena Lingard framed in a doorway at the beginning of the second book and later in Lincoln, combine the costume realism and impressionistic light and color of the American painters: "I did not recognize her until she stepped into the light of my doorway and I beheld—Lena Lingard! . . . Her black suit fitted her figure smoothly, and a black lace hat, with pale-blue forget-me-nots, sat demurely on her yellow hair" (265). Cather's sensitivity to the accomplishments of these native painters is evident in her commentary on Chase's "What Did You Say?" in "A Philistine in a Gallery" (1900): "Young Art Student[s] . . . score [Chase] because he has the trick of color, and because his pictures are pleasing to the eye and convey no lofty message. Mr. Chase . . . is an admirable colorist, and he believes that there is a sort of divinity in color itself. . . . A pretty little girl, daintily posed in a studio, painted with beautiful refinement of color, has . . . a right to exist in the catholic kingdom of art. . . ."

Jim Burden, like his creator, is fascinated with picture-making, and his memoir contains an abundance of portraits, genre paintings, and landscapes. Among the memorable portraits are those of Otto Fuchs, the elder Burdens, Mr. Shimerda (who resembles "the old portraits [Jim] remembered in Virginia" [24]), Mrs. Harling, and the Cutters. It can be argued that the tradition of genre painting in America conditions Jim's way of seeing and recalling his experiences. Genre painting, or painting of the people, frequently mentioned in the following commentary section, depicts group scenes from daily life, is sometimes narrative in intent, and frequently sentimental. While the genre instinct was prevalent among anonymous and primitive painters, genre subject matter is obvious in artists like Homer, Thomas Eakins, Millet, and Pierre Auguste Renoir, and Cather's writings on painting indicate much fascination with genre. In the 1895 review she praises genre studies by Flavia Canfield, the mother of her friend Dorothy, especially one called "Soldiers," a picture of two Salvation Army women "sad without being painful. There is a good deal of expression worked into the faces. The picture is sympathetic without being prosy and tells the story without obtruding it." In "A Philistine in a Gallery" she singles out "Madonna and Child" by Josef Israels, a Dutch genre painter: "The simplicity of its directness and treatment . . . are in no-wise lost upon the Philistine . . . , though [Israels's] technique was the best of one of the best schools in all the history of painting." About Gari Melchers's "Sailor and His Sweetheart" she says: "One who has seen the woman can never forget her, the robust uncorseted figure, the heavy, thick hands with blunt fingers." In a related 1901 review she likes Marianne Stokes's "Little Brother and Sister," an illustration of the old Brothers Grimm fairy tale about children driven into the forest by their stepmother.

The genre tradition informs Jim's ways of seeing and arranging what he sees. For example, the novel opens with a classic genre description of the Shimerda family illumined in the red glow from the fire-box of a locomotive: "A group of people stood huddled together on the platform, encumbered by bundles and boxes. . . . The woman wore a fringed shawl tied over her head, and she carried a little tin trunk in her arms, hugging it as if it were a baby. There was an old man, tall and stooped. Two half-grown boys and a girl stood holding oilcloth bundles, and a little girl clung to her mother's skirts" (5–6). At the other end of the novel, Jim looks back at the Cuzak family as he rides down the hill to the gate: "The group [the little ones looked at me with friendly faces] was still there by the windmill. Ántonia was waving her apron" (368). Genre instinct is evident in Jim's description of the Burden hired hands sitting in the kitchen: "I can still see these two men sitting on the bench; Otto's close-clipped head and Jake's shaggy hair slicked flat in front by a wet comb. I can see the sag of their tired shoulders against the whitewashed wall" (67). The interior of the Shimerda dugout is classic genre: "The old man was sitting on the stump behind a stove, crouching over as if he were trying to hide from us. Yulka was on the floor at his feet, her kitten in her lap. . . . Ántonia was washing pans and dishes in a dark corner. The crazy boy lay under the only window, stretched on a gunny-sack stuffed with straw" (73). Although it is a moving rather than still picture, Mr. Shimerda's funeral, with the group of mourners singing and praying in the snow near the open grave, can be classified as genre, as can the children huddling beneath the painted glass window of the church during the Black Hawk winter, the hired girls dancing to Blind d'Arnault's playing, and even the scenes in Lena's parlor and the performance of the stage play in Lincoln.

After the strategic third book Jim's pictorial sense increases to a fascination with poses. The setting he describes for Widow Steavens's story of Ántonia's fall prepares us for the final book's numerous pictorial stills. "All the windows were open" in Mrs. Steavens's old sitting-room, he notes. "The white summer moon was shining outside, the windmill was pumping lazily in the light breeze. My hostess put the lamp on a stand in the corner, and turned it low because of the heat. She sat down in her favourite rocking-chair and settled a little stool comfortably under her feet" (307). Later, when Jim approaches the Cuzak farm he notes "a wide farm-house, with a red barn and an ash grove, and cattleyards. . . ." Then his eye focuses on two boys in a plum thicket beside the road bending over a dead dog: "The little one, not more than four or five, was on his knees, his hands folded, and his close-clipped, bare head drooping forward in deep dejection. The other stood beside him, a hand on his shoulder, and was comforting him in a language I had not heard in a long while" (329). The same sentimental genre art is evident when the little boy appeals to Ántonia for comfort in his loss: "He stood by her chair, leaning his elbows on her knees and twisting her apron strings in his slender fingers while he told her his story in Bohemian, and the tears brimmed over and hung on his long lashes. His mother listened, spoke soothingly to him and in a whisper promised him something that made him give her a quick, teary smile" (336). A family concert gotten up for Jim is the subject of another genre picture, with Leo struggling with a violin too big for him while Nina does her "pretty little dance on the boards with her bare feet" (348). Jim's picture of Leo and Ambrosch in the hayloft the next morning recalls Homer's "Boys in a Pasture": "long bands of sunshine were coming in at the window and reaching back under the eaves where the two boys lay. Leo was wide awake and was tickling his brother's leg with a dried cone-flower he had pulled out of the hay. Ambrosch kicked at him and turned over. . . . Leo lay on his back, elevated one foot, and began exercising his toes.

He picked up dried flowers with his toes and brandished them in the belt of sunlight. After he had amused himself thus for some time, he rose on one elbow and began to look at me, cautiously, then critically, blinking his eyes in the light. His expression was droll; it dismissed me lightly" (354).

More important than either portraiture or genre art in *My Ántonia* is landscape painting, a tradition in America encompassing many movements and of which Cather was well aware. In a 1901 review on the Chicago Art Institute she appreciates the light in "Prairie Fire" by George Inness, the most hybrid of American painters, influenced at various times by the Hudson River school, luminism, the Barbizon painters, and impressionism. Cather also praises Robinson's "Scene on the Delaware and Hudson Canal" in her 1895 review, commenting on the "bracing, exhilarating effect" of its "air and sunlight, its abundance of clear atmosphere. . . ." She criticizes Richard Lorenz's "In the West," in the same Lincoln exhibit, for its "unwestern atmosphere," indicating her fascination with attempts to capture sunlight: "the impressionists say it is 'keyed too low.' Whatever that may mean the lights are certainly at fault and the color is too tame. The sunlight is gentle, not the fierce, white, hot sunlight of the West. Sunlight on the plains is almost like sunlight of the northern seas; it is a glaring, irritating, shelterless light that makes the atmosphere throb and pulsate with heat."

Considering these comments, it is not surprising that impressionistic renderings of landscape are prevalent in this novel. Many of Jim's landscape descriptions, although they are the products of memory (which is not a characteristic of impressionism), give the effect of spontaneity and movement and emphasize primary colors or their complements in bold strokes. Although such color is absent in the opening description of Jim's night ride across the prairie, the emphasis is on response and movement: he *feels* the terrain to be "slightly undulating . . . because often our wheels ground against the brake as we went down into a hollow and lurched up again on the other side" (7). His view of fields during his walk to the Burden garden adds color and is a clear example of verbal impressionism. After conveying the landscape's rough texture, he emphasizes shaggy, wine-red grass broken by box-elder trees turning yellow. Movement is added as the grass bends to the wind: "I felt motion in the landscape; in the fresh, easy-blowing morning wind, and in the earth itself, as if the shaggy grass were a sort of loose hide, and underneath it herds of wild buffalo were galloping, galloping . . ." (16). On the way to the Shimerdas' in the third chapter Jim creates another, albeit brief, landscape picture. From the moving wagon he sees the "broken, grassy clay cliffs which indicated the windings of the stream, and the glittering tops of the cottonwood and ash trees that grew down in the ravine. Some of the cottonwoods had already turned, and the yellow leaves and shining white bark made them look like the gold and silver trees in fairy tales" (21). In the next chapter, after noting Mormon sunflower trails that lend color to the undulating prairie of moving grass, he describes the "rich copper color" of smartweed accenting the "pale-yellow cornfields" (29). The opening of the ninth chapter contains an impressionistic sketch of a winter landscape: a metallic sky above blonde cornfields fades to "ghostliness" behind big whirling flakes of snow which deposit on the grass like "strokes of Chinese white on canvas" (62). During the sleigh ride the stretches of prairie are blinding in the sunlight; the few cedars stand out in "strong, dusky green," and the ghostly cornfields transform to the "palest possible gold in sun and snow" (64). Such descriptions are evident throughout, although decreasingly, as I indicate below.

The second book opens with a view of Black Hawk from the upstairs window of Jim's house in town, which, while deficient in color, implies it in the "winding line of river bluffs" and in the "brick" store buildings, school-house, and court-house contrasting with "green yards" and "white" fences and churches (145). More typically impressionistic is Jim's landscape toward the end of this book, during his ride to the river to picnic with the hired girls: "The pink bee-bush stood tall along the sandy roadsides, and the cone-flowers and rose mallow grew everywhere. Across the wire fence, in the long grass, I saw a clump of flaming orange-coloured milkweed, rare in that part of the state. I left the road and went around through a stretch of pasture that was always cropped short in summer where the gaillardia came up year after year and matted over the ground with the deep, velvety red that is in Bokhara carpets" (232–33). In most of these descriptions there is a rapid noting of the appearances of an objective world; that is, they are mimetic presentations of what the beholder experiences and very much in the tradition of American impressionism as illustrations of place (like the paintings of Robinson, Childe Hassam, John Henry Twachtman, and late Inness—subject matter is never secondary as in the French tradition. These descriptions, although filtered through memory, are uncolored by sentiment; in them Cather's and Jim's "views" essentially coincide.

The landscapes more memorable to readers reveal acquaintance with another, more romantic American tradition, that of luminism, which Cather uses to clothe landscapes with sentiment and sometimes distinguish her vision from the character Jim's when his becomes colored by feelings she might not share. Like the impressionists, the luminists' interests were atmosphere and light; however, instead of communicating motion or momentary appearance, luminists attempted to freeze time and clothe scenes with feeling. Barbara Novak aptly characterizes luminism as a "poetic rather than analytic approach" to nature. "If we say that Impressionism is the *objective* response to the *visual* sensation of light, then perhaps we can say that luminism is the *poetic* response to the *felt* sensation." This approach evolved from the conflict between the real and ideal evident in the landscapes of Thomas Cole, between his own preference for imaginatively rendered landscapes filtered through memory and the public's demand for specific views objectively rendered. Cole's method to look intently on an object for a period of time and then go to his studio and paint it, "employing memory," Novak notes, "as an aesthetic component," relates to Cather's statement that "Life began for me when I ceased to admire and began to remember." In the process, "Cole tended to dispose nature's parts according to an *a-priori* sense of composition . . . [and rely for] details of American scenery upon formulae derived from earlier prototypes, or upon his own favorite compositional schemes. . . ." Although Cather, like Cole, relied on memory and filtered her memories through literary and painterly prototypes, in *My Ántonia* she did so partially as a strategy for characterization.

Jim's most memorable landscapes resemble the paintings of the luminists (like Asher B. Durand, John F. Kensett, Martin Johnson Heade), who solved Cole's real–ideal polarity by rendering nature objectively while romanticizing it through light and atmosphere. Sunrise and especially sunset were times of day favored by these painters to depict objects with more clarity than they would have outside a painting while allowing the intensifying light to dazzle from a distant core where it envelops detail in atmosphere. Cather approximates this technique when her vision and Jim's seem to coincide (as in the appearance of Mr. Shimerda at sunset and in the plow passage at the end of the second book) and where Jim's vision diverges from hers (as in the farewell scene in the fourth book). Before Shimerda appears as a figure at the edge of the upland in the first book, luminous heightening of reality is evident in "the miles of copper-red grass ... drenched in sunlight ... stronger and fiercer than at any other time of the day," and in the rose haystacks throwing long shadows. The enveloping of the landscape in dazzling light is evident in the prairie appearing "like the bush that burned with fire and was not consumed. That hour always had the exaltation of victory, of triumphant ending, like a hero's death ... it was a sudden transfiguration, a lifting up of day" (40). Jim's recollection of this childhood moment is colored by the sadness associated with autumn weather and knowledge of the impending suicide of the old man and makes this landscape far different from earlier ones.

More expressive, I think, of Cather's own sentiments is the sunset at the end of "The Hired Girls." In it the transfiguring light of luminism has less subjective overtones. The poeticizing light here expresses and creates an intensely magic moment, the emotionalism of which is contained in the scene itself rather than transferred to it from the outside. The grass is afire, the barks of trees "red as copper" the sandbars "glittered like glass," and movement gives way to the freezing of time characteristic of luminism: the "light trembl[ing] in the willow thickets as if little flames were leaping among them" is arrested when the "breeze sank to stillness." Defined rays of sunlight evident in painters like Jasper Francis Cropsey and Frederic Edwin Church are present here in the "long fingers of the sun touch[ing the girls'] foreheads." The intensely delineated object is the plow encircled within but not dazzled by the red disk sun: "it stood out against the sun, was exactly contained within the circle of the disk, the handles, the tongue, the share—black against the molten red. There it was, heroic in size, a picture writing on the sun" (244–45). This is, undoubtedly, the novel's supreme luminist scene.

A corruption of luminism, as in some of the landscapes of Church and Albert Bierstadt, whose paintings, claims Novak, "involved to some degree parodies of high-mindedness and a magnification of popular taste," is apparent in Jim's farewell scene with Ántonia in the fourth book. From Cather's perspective, the scene is parody, the product of sentimentality. Time is suspended: the sun "hung there [until] the moon rose in the east . . . for five, perhaps ten minutes the two luminaries confronted each other across the level land, resting on opposite edges of the world" (321–22). In this "singular light" details in the landscape are surrealistically singled out: "every little tree and shock of wheat, every sunflower stalk and clump of snow-on-the-mountain, drew itself up high and pointed; the very clods and furrows in the fields seemed to stand up sharply." As I will explain in the following commentary, these excesses, like Bierstadt's postcard pink skies, amount to deceptions, are meant to color over the realities implied in Jim's confession that "our ways parted" and "I went back alone . . ." (322–23).

My Ántonia comes to us, then, as the product of a persona intimately acquainted with the arts. Jim's memoir is indebted to a variety of other works and traditions that function as an alembic for the raw materials of Cather's life. The *Georgics* provides the image of the plow, the plowed-up sword, the fruitful earth, the summer storm, the snake, the sick horse, winter interiors, and the final picture of Ántonia as the idealized country person. The novel's themes of sex and breeding, simple virtues, toil, development of civilization, poeticizing humble life, and loss and restoration are also anticipated in the *Georgics*.

Biblical and mythological echoes complement these themes and images, and Dumas's play mirrors the relationship between Jim and Lena in book 3. Music and especially painterly traditions and styles contribute to Jim's method of communicating feeling and viewing his past in ways to give his life meaning.

6

Textual Commentary

The introduction to *My Ántonia* emphasizes Cather's separation from her narrator, Jim Burden, a character in his own right, and suggests the quiet despair, even desperation, of his unfruitful life. Behind the sketchy portrait of Ántonia, the benign "central figure" who "seemed to mean to [Jim and Cather] the country, the conditions, the adventure of [their] childhood," lurks the sinister figure of Jim's wife, "unimpressionable and temperamentally incapable of enthusiasm," irritated by her husband's "quiet tastes." Cather's comment that Jim's "romantic disposition . . . often made him seem very funny as a boy" gives notice to the reader that this memoir will be colored by feelings and imagination, a creative rather than realistic portrait to the title of which Jim affixes the possessive pronoun "My." Cather's persona also establishes her own fondness for the girl they both knew: "He made me see her again, feel her presence, revived all my old affection for her." In sharp contrast is her curious confession regarding Mrs. James Burden: "I do not like his wife." These three simply written pages in italicized print suggest what to keep in mind while we read the five books that follow.

Book 1, "The Shimerdas"

The emphasis in this book is on exile and toil; everyone comes from a more comfortable elsewhere and is challenged by unfamiliar terrain and hostile environment. The result is the slow and sometimes painful evolution of civilization on the prairie. Jim Burden's model is the first two books of Virgil's *Georgics*, which tell of human lapse from a golden age of ease and fruitful soil owing to Jove's decree that man must labor, "that the path of tillage be not smooth" (1:121), that man be set against beast ("He put fell poison in the serpent's fang, / Bade wolves to prowl . . ." [1:129–30]), that fire be hidden away, etc. As in the expulsion from Eden, man has to struggle to survive, to tame and hunt beasts, plow the earth, develop tools, etc. But man can never rest on his accomplishments. Weather, blight, the inclination to decline demand constant effort for survival:

> So it is: for everything by nature's law
> Tends to the worse, slips ever backward, backward
> As with a man who scarce propels his boat
> Against the stream; if once his arms relax,
> The current sweeps it headlong down the rapids.
>
> (1:200–4)

Because man must be vigilant, Virgil includes weather forecasting and seasonal challenges, details the care and suitable soils needed for various crops and trees—black crumbly soil is best for corn; olives must be provided with sufficient moisture to swell to plumpness, etc.

Space of Exile After identifying himself as without mother and father and briefly describing Ántonia and her family in painterly fashion (illuminated by the glow from the locomotive fire box), which he must do at the start because of her important role in his memoir, Jim turns his attention to the terrain. His recollection of his response to Nebraska is impressionistic, focusing on perception: "There seemed to be nothing to see. . . . If there was a road, I could not make it out in the faint starlight. . . . Nothing but land—slightly undulating, I knew, because often our wheels ground against the brake as we went down into a hollow and lurched up again on the other side" (7). Jim briefly recalls Virginia, his "elsewhere," but then surrenders himself to an experience for which he has no models—his "Life of Jesse James" failing to prepare him for the reality of his own Western experience or enable him to read correctly the character of Otto Fuchs, who "might have stepped out of the pages of 'Jesse James'" (6) but proves totally unlike his demeanor. (However, we should note here Jim's early compulsion to view reality from literary models.) He is unconditioned for "nothing but land: not a country at all, but the material out of which countries are made" (7), and he feels "erased, blotted out" (8).

Jim gives the second chapter much the same structure as the first, moving from characters to landscape. After recalling waking up (being reborn?) in this new environment, he introduces his lively, hard-working grandmother and his patriarchal, Bible-reading grandfather, who intones Psalm 47, about God extending his kingdom to all peoples. Jim recalls running out-of-doors, noticing slopes, gulleys, and draws in the immediate vicinity, and then the great cornfield on the western horizon. Besides the corn, a sorghum patch and a few rusty willows, "Everywhere . . . there was nothing but rough, shaggy, red grass . . ." (14). The blowing grass gives motion to the landscape, makes it alive, and it has the color of wine stains, doubtlessly an influence from Homer. The various stages of humans on the land are suggested in the catalog of prairie dwellings: the dugout represents the first stage of civilization, followed by soddies and then by houses above ground, like the Burden dwelling. The existence of a garden on the land, which Jim visits with his grandmother to fetch potatoes, augments this pattern of development, and references to snakes and a friendly badger indicate man's fall from better fortunes as well as his loneliness.

The vastness of this scene of the boy and the old woman on the faint path to the windswept garden is a poignant introduction to Jim's romantic fantasies of floating like the hawks into sun and sky. When his grandmother leaves him alone, leaning against a warm yellow pumpkin, he experiences complete happiness, the feeling of being dissolved into the universal, "whether it is sun and air, or goodness and knowledge" (18). The experience recalls the transparent eye-ball passage at the beginning of *Nature*, when alone in the woods Emerson feels the currents of the Universal Being circulating through him, and also the later passage where he admits a child's love of nature: "I expand and live in the warm day like corn and melons." Jim approaches this new world with new eyes, as Emerson encourages, building his own world, his own heaven.

During his ride to the Shimerda place in the next chapter (3), Jim notes the roughening landscape near Squaw Creek—grassy clay cliffs above a ravine of cottonwoods and ash, then rugged red hillocks and draws as he approaches the dugout. The Bohemians, among them the animal-like Marek, emerge one by one through their door in the earth, anticipating the lively explosion of life from Ántonia's fruit cave in the novel's final book. The fourteen-year-old Ántonia is painted in appropriate earth tones, has eyes like sunlight on brown water, brown skin and hair, and dark cheeks. Jim now begins to view the landscape in conjunction with her, linking the girl and the country as the introduction indicates. He and Antonia followed by little Yulka race about in celebration of open spaces and then settle in the tall red grass, naming and associating objects in the environment about them: "She pointed up to the sky, then to my eyes, then back to the sky" (26) to learn the word for the color blue.

After being taught new words, Ántonia offers Jim a silver ring, indicative of their union at the end of the novel, but he refuses it, repulsing her "quite sternly. I didn't want her ring, and felt there was something reckless and extravagant about her wishing to give it away to a boy she had never seen before" (27). He is quickly "engaged," however, when the girl's father "ordains" him with a laying on of hands to teach "my Ántonia." The sky–earth, male–female, Jim–Ántonia counterpoise established during this language lesson is repeated at the end of the fourth book with the sun and moon resting on opposite edges of the world, the "pale silver" moon recalling the little silver ring offered by Ántonia and rejected, but now accepted in Jim's intention "always to carry with me; the closest, realist face, under all the shadows of women's faces, at the bottom of my memory" (322).

Humanity's evolution from the earth and toward language is thus clarified during the visit to the Shimerdas'. Paralleling the dugout dwellers are the prairie dogs and earth owls observed by the children. To Jim, the owls, as winged creatures, and men are degraded in dwelling beneath the earth, and he comments on the deterioration of domestic life such primitive conditions force upon the Shimerdas.

Darkening Dimensions   A combination of cold, evil, and enmity between man and beast begins to darken Jim's story. The hated Peter Krajiek, who exploits and lives off the Shimerdas, is associated with the rattlesnakes terrorizing the prairie-dogs and owls beneath the ground, and Jim introduces the Russians, Peter and Pavel, who have been exiled because of their part in the horrible wolves episode. The story of these Russians begins disarmingly as one of Jim's painterly set pieces—a neat log house with a well by the door and surrounded by ripe melons, squashes, and cucumbers. Peter plays the wife to the glum and sickly Pavel, does the washing, makes the beds, cares for the cow, and sees to the food, while Pavel works out. (They are one of several male couples in Cather, anticipating Tom Outland and Roddy Blake in *The Professor's House*, Claude Wheeler and David Gerhardt in *One of Ours*, and Fathers Latour and Vaillant in *Death Comes for the Archbishop*.) These Russians provide a refuge for old Mr. Shimerda, who grows increasingly depressed as winter approaches. Similar dark themes are prevalent in the *Georgics*, in which the threat of snakes and wolves reminds man of his fallen state, and the trials of winter in the northern steppes are vividly described.

Old Mr. Shimerda's depression is evident on the day when Jim discovers ice on the pond and the asparagus stalks fallen into a slimy mass, and when Ántonia warms a frozen insect in her hair until it is able to chirp, a detail that relates to her salutary effect on her father while it brings the Old World closer through the story of Hata, a singing Bohemian beggar. To prepare for the old man's entrance Jim paints a spectacular sunset, enveloping the prairie in dazzling light and shadow: "miles of copper, red grass . . . drenched in sunlight . . . , cornfields [in] red gold, hay stacks . . . rosy and [throwing] long shadows" (40). Before this glorious light, in which his and Ántonia's shadows flit beside them on the grass, Jim places Mr. Shimerda's silhouette, "moving on the edge of the upland, a gun over his shoulder. He was walking slowly, dragging his feet along as if he had no purpose" (41). Here is another American literary echo, of the melancholy figure of the exiled and soon-to-die Natty Bumppo as he appears within the fiery disk of sun at the beginning of James Fenimore Cooper's *The Prairie*, a sunset image we are reminded of later in the celebrated description of the colossal plow against the sun in the second book. Ántonia runs to her father and temporarily revives him: "She was the only one of his family who could rouse the old man from the torpor in which he seemed to live" (41); however, his smile remains "full of sadness, of pity for things" (42). This scene ends with Jim racing his shadow home in the sudden cold. Shadows here, first two and then one, underscore the darkening dimensions, suggest the companionship of Ántonia and Jim, and anticipate their farewell scene at the end of the fourth book, when Jim leaves his friend and returns alone to town.

The snake, referred to consistently up to now, comes with the wolf to the foreground in a pair of chapters (7 and 8) that precipitate the first book toward its climax. Much has been made of both chapters relative to Jim's unhappy marriage and his failure to develop a satisfying sexual relationship with Ántonia. The snake episode is definitely sexist, establishing in Jim's mind his superiority to Ántonia, who is merely a girl, but its sexuality is more debatable. Recent critics interpret what Jim calls his "mock adventure" (49) as a burrowing into the unconsciousness, a confrontation with repressed images that become overt in book 3 when Jim struggles with Ántonia's would-be rapist, Wick Cutter. If we associate the snake with the phallus, Jim's queasy response to it does betray sexual disgust leading to abnegation of sex in his own life, although the snake, as Jim indicates, relates to "ancient, eldest Evil" (47), which has more than sexual overtones. In the third book of the *Georgics*, the book from which Jim later quotes, the snake is branded a curse, life-threatening to man, his domestic beasts, and his progress. Virgil advises that the snake be killed:

> Quick, herdsman, pick up a stone, pick up a stick,
> And as he rears his swelling, hissing throat
> To threaten, down with him!
>
> (3:420–22)

The complete passage of twenty-six lines contains many details similar to those in Jim's graphic description of the old rattler. Virgil notes the snake's coils, writhing tail, slow curves, tortuous scaly back, mottled and blotched belly, rolling and blazing eyes, and three-forked flickering tongue. Jim notes the "abominable muscularity" and "fluid motion," the tightening coils and wavy loops, green ooze from the hideous head (45–47). Although the snake killing is an initiation experience for Jim, one that causes Ántonia, for a time at least, to regard him as "just like big mans" (46), we must look beyond this personal aspect to the fallen condition of humanity the threatening snake has come to symbolize. The echoes of Genesis are clear as Jim confronts the snake. He observes that "Ántonia, barefooted as she was, ran up behind me" (46). Recall the words to the tempter: "I will make you enemies of each other: you and the woman, your offspring and her offspring. It will crush your head and you will strike its heel" (3:15).

The Russian wolves episode further develops darkening dimensions. Although the wolf is mentioned in the *Georgics* as a threat and a reminder of humanity's fallen state, Virgil does not give it the extended treatment he gives the snake. Cather doubtlessly was influenced by the Paul Powis painting of attacking wolves that hung in the Webster County Courthouse during her childhood and was later discovered in a Red Cloud closet; additionally she would have known the folklore of man-eating wolves. By distancing us from the wolves in time, place, and even language, she leaves room for the imagination to increase their haunting quality. "For Ántonia and me," writes Jim, "the story of the wedding party was never at an end. . . . At night, before I went to sleep, I often found myself in a sledge drawn by three horses, dashing through a country that looked something like Nebraska and something like Virginia" (61).

Jim links this episode to the snake killing in an angular but definite way, by establishing a connection between the Russians and the wicked Black Hawk money lender, Wick Cutter, and by associating his first encounter with the snake, discovered "lying in long loose waves, like a letter 'W'" (45). Cutter is part of the misfortune "which seemed to settle like an evil bird on the roof of the [Russians'] log house, and to flap its wings there, warning human beings away" (51). Other ominous details preface the telling of the tale: the weather suddenly turns cold, Ántonia and Jim reflect upon the power of the stars over men's destinies, coyotes howl, wind, "singing through big spaces," beats on the windows and brings to mind defeated armies and restless ghosts (53).

The description of the telling itself in a language Jim cannot understand recalls in its method his initial impressionistic description of the prairie. The focus is on Jim's impressions of Pavel's contempt toward Peter, of his excitement and rage, and of the effect of these on Ántonia, who is able to understand what is being related and clasps Jim's hand under the table (54–55). The actual tale reflects Jim's penchant for aesthetically ordering even unpleasant experiences and is beautifully structured, hung between the jolly festivities of the wedding supper and the ringing of the Angelus bell at the monastery—at both ends a dramatic contrast to the horror of the overturned sledges and the sacrificing of the bride and the groom. Those bent on a sexual reading of the novel will find significance in Pavel's decision to toss away the bride, although to see this as the essence of the episode amounts to distortion. Death in pursuit, objectified in the dark shadows of the animals moving swiftly over the snow and in Pavel's savage efforts to escape death, which comes to him a few days after he unburdens his soul to Shimerda, testifies to the ancient eldest evil implicit in the snake and in "horrible unconscious memories in all warm-blooded life" (47). The threat of snake and wolf thus moves from the external world to deep within the human psyche.

Winter Paintings Winter arrives in chapter 9 with a prairie snowstorm that Jim describes impressionistically, continuing the tone of Pavel's story in "the blond cornfields [fading] out into ghostliness at

Paul Powis painting displayed in Webster County Courthouse during Cather's childhood.
Nebraska State Historical Society

last" (62). The effect of snow on the large circular mark in the grass where the Indians raced horses becomes, with "the first light spray of snow . . . over it, . . . like strokes of Chinese white on canvas." Jim's calling attention to the circle, which he considers—ironically, in light of the approaching death of Mr. Shimerda—as "a good omen for the winter," betrays the therapeutic impulse behind his memoir, which he clarifies at the end as a "coming home to myself, . . . having found out what a little circle man's experience is" (371–72). Descriptions of the snow-covered landscape continue during a sleigh ride with the Shimerda girls, another echo of the story of the macabre ride across the snow in Russia. Jim's subsequent convalescence from quinsy occasions a contrasting genre painting of the basement kitchen as "a tight little boat in a winter sea" (65), full of good things to eat and offering refuge for the tired men whose hands are numbed and cracked with cold. He recalls popping corn and making taffy in this protected place while the hired men sing cowboy songs and tell animal stories. His description of Jake and Otto seated on a bench, "the sag of their tired shoulders against the whitewashed wall" (67), easing their boots while he and his grandmother wash the dishes, introduces a eulogy to these faithful workers and also the humorous story of Otto's trip from Austria with a woman charge who gave birth to triplets, a story that illustrates his good nature and anticipates Ántonia's breeding capacities.

Virgil provides the model for Jim's (and Cather's) winter interiors and landscape paintings, noting in the *Georgics* that "when it's cold outside / Farmers enjoy their gains and give themselves / To mutual entertainment" (1:300–2), and hunters "live at ease deep underground, / Secure in dugouts, warmed by logs they pile, / . . . / The night they spend in games . . ." (3:376–79). The hardships of the season, which Cather emphasizes in her next chapter, are also acknowledged by Virgil:

> . . . far and wide
> The land lies shapeless under drifts of snow
> And piles of ice full seven cubits high.
> Winter is endless [on the steppes], and nor'-west winds

Whistle with endless cold; nor does the sun
Ever disperse the pall of pallid fog
. . . .
Whole ponds are found turned into solid ice
And uncombed beards bristle with icicles.
Meanwhile the air is no less thick with snow;
Beasts perish, frozen stiff huge shapes of oxen
Stand starkly round, and huddling herds of deer
Lurk paralyzed beneath fresh drifts of snow,
Their antlers barely showing.

(3:354–57, 365–71)

Toil is evident in the picture of a farmer

Who sits up late in winter and by firelight
With a sharp blade trims his torches, while his wife,
Singing to mitigate her drudgery,
Passes the piercing shuttle through the web,
Or boiling down sweet must [new wine] over the hearth
Skims froth with a bunch of leaves from the bubbling
    cauldron.

(1:291–96)

The picture of the Shimerda family provides a contrast to winter life at the Burdens'. Jim once again paints a genre interior, this time of the dark depressing dugout the Bohemians call home:

The old man was sitting on a stump behind the stove, crouching over as if he were trying to hide from us. Yulka was on the floor at his feet, her kitten in her lap. . . . Ántonia was washing pans and dishes in a dark corner. The crazy boy lay under the only window, stretched on a gunny sack stuffed with straw. . . . The air in the cave was stifling, and it was very dark, too. A lighted lantern, hung over the stove, threw out a feeble yellow glimmer. (73)

The reactions of Ántonia's parents to these conditions—the accusatory sorrow of the mother, the wounded self-respect of the father—illustrate how hardship can warp character. Also of significance are Ántonia's sleeping place and the gift of dried mushrooms. The hole scooped out of the black earth, in light of Ántonia's association with the fruitful earth, suggests Persephone's annual sojourn in the underworld, or winter itself. Response to the mushrooms, memorable for their look, odor, and taste—and for Jim's later recognition of their identity (a detail like the taste of tea and cake in Proust's *Swann's Way,* which generates the image of an early experience)—illustrates the suspicion and misunderstanding of foreigners of which even good people like the Burdens are guilty.

Jim's ability to pattern his memories is evident in the climactic chapters (11 to 16) of this first and longest book; he creates in essence a diptych framed in snow—actually blizzards. The first big winter storm occurs four days before Christmas, obliterates the landscape, and cuts the Burden family off from town. During this time Jim prepares a scrapbook for Yulka and pastes in as frontispiece "Napoleon Announcing the Divorce to Josephine" (a detail seen recently, like Pavel's sacrificing of the bride, as an antiwoman, antimarriage element), and Otto and Grandmother Burden make candles and prepare a box of goodies for the Bohemians. All help decorate the little cedar Jake cuts down for Jim, Otto providing the creche figures. These stiff cardboard cutouts include the Christ child, singing angels, the three kings, and the bleeding heart—a symbol of Christ's love. Christmas day begins with Grandfather Burden reading Matthew's account of the Nativity, continues with feasting and dominoes, and concludes with a thank-you visit from Mr. Shimerda, who causes some disturbance by kneeling before the candle-lit tree. More pointedly than the rejection of mushrooms, the elder Burden's "Protestantizing the atmosphere" (87) illustrates the undercurrent of cultural tensions. Narrator and, consequently, reader view a foreign, Catholic culture as alien in America. After this half of the diptych, the snow melts—the frame closes: "The soft black earth stood out in patches along the roadsides" (88). Jim's extended description of the feuding bulls during the thaw might be an anticipation of the sexual themes of the second and third books and also another borrowing from Virgil, who describes bulls in the mating season as

charging alternately
In violent battle. Many a wound is opened,
Dark blood streams down their sides, and horn to horn
They butt each other bellowing terribly,
Till woods and sky from end to end re-echo.

(3:219–23)

There follows a brief altercation between Jim and Ántonia when she and her mother visit the Burdens to complain about their need compared to their neighbors' plenty. Then, on the twentieth of January, as the winter's biggest snow begins to fall, a new frame opens for the second half of the diptych, to enclose a picture of death. News arrives that old Shimerda has killed himself in his barn, in surroundings recalling the Christmas story. We need not explore the gruesome details provided by Otto, although it should be noted that Jim and the reader are distanced from this disaster (as they are from Ántonia's ruin described in the third book). What is important is that the birth of Christ has been juxtaposed with an old man's death on the prairie and that both are framed in snow. As if to underscore this connection, Jake's description of the pathetic situation at the Shimerdas' is included: a lighted lantern is kept over the corpse, still housed with horses and oxen, and Ántonia, her mother, and brother kneel beneath the lantern (as the old man had knelt before the Christmas tree) to pray for the suicide's soul. Details emphasizing the frozen, contorted corpse, its head bandaged like a mummy's—the novel's primary image of death—set it against the stiff cardboard cutout of the Christ Child Jim hangs on the cedar tree. There are echoes here of Paul's proclamation that through Christ "all men will be brought to life; Death came through one man and in the same way the resurrection of the dead has come through one man" (1 Cor. 15:21–23). While the approaching spring will bring one level of resurrection, resurrection in the fullest sense must wait until the final pages of the novel when Jim witnesses the explosion of children from Ántonia's cave.

Because suicide causes concern about the condition of a soul dying out of grace, there follows a debate over the need for a priest, for burial in consecrated ground, the doctrine of Purgatory, etc. Again, lines are drawn between Catholic and Protestant traditions as the young Bohemian Anton Jelinek relates his experience in helping a priest distribute Communion to dying soldiers during a cholera epidemic. Jelinek's story reflects literalism toward Christ's discourse at Capernaum: "As I, who am sent by the living Father, myself draw life from the Father, so whoever eats me will draw life from me. This is bread come down from heaven; . . . anyone who eats this bread will live forever" (John 6:57–58). There is a connection between the Christmas story (the bread coming from heaven) and the dead who await resurrection (who will live forever). Jim's contemplation and dismissal of the belief in Purgatory and his curiosity about the location of Mr. Shimerda's soul, which he feels is lingering in the comfortable Burden sitting-room, is both part of this general discussion and a link to the earlier Pavel episode, when he imagined the wind to be ghosts seeking shelter from the howling waste (53). All is brought to rest in Mr. Burden's prayer at the burial: "Oh, great and just God, no man among us knows what the sleeper knows, nor is it for us to judge what lies between him and Thee" (117). The diptych is capped with Jim's comment on the grave at the crossroads as "the spot most dear to me" in "all that country" (119).

Spring and Summer Finale

Jim's memoir omits the months between January and spring, thus dramatizing the contrast between winter's darkest experience and renewal of life—"spring itself; the throb of it, the light restlessness, the vital essence . . ." (120). The Shimerdas emerge from the earth into an above-ground log house, and Ántonia takes to the fields. Her affinity with the earth is now exaggerated: "her arms and throat were burned as brown as a sailor's. Her neck came up strongly out of her shoulders, like the bole of a tree out of the turf, . . . that draught-horse neck [of] the peasant" (122). Although these qualities seem negative ones to Jim, they confirm her as Persephone emerged from the underworld to spend her time on earth with her corn goddess mother, Demeter. The fruitfulness of the earth is the dominant theme of these chapters (17 to 19): "breathless, brilliant heat . . . makes the plains of Kansas and Nebraska the best corn country in the world. It seemed as if we could hear the corn growing in the night; under the stars one caught a faint crackling in the dewy, heavy-odoured cornfields where the feathered stalks stood so juicy and green" (137). Virgil again provides the model:

> in spring the country swells
> Clamouring for the fertilizing seeds.
> Then the almighty father Heaven descends
> Into the lap of his rejoicing bride
> With fecund showers, and with her mighty body
> Mingling in might begets all manner of fruits.
> . . . .
> The nurturing earth is pregnant; warmed by breezes
> Of Zephyrus the fields unloose their bosoms.
> (2:324–32)

This optimism is somewhat marred when difficulties arise between Jim and Ántonia and their families, a discord introduced during the thaw after Christmas and continued here in the horse-collar incident when Jake knocks down Ambrosch, and Ántonia shouts, "I never like you no more, Jake and Jim Burden . . . no friends any more!" (130). Grandfather Burden quiets these petty differences by curing the Shimerdas' horse of colic and not taking full payment for a cow he sold them. (The details of the sick horse might owe something to Virgil's long passage on sick horses and cattle in georgic 3 [see, for example, 492–526].) Also, Jim seems aware that Ántonia's rejection of schooling and her boasts about being like a man shield a more sensitive side, expressed in her request that he not forget her father. When Jim wonders why she fails to be "nice" all the time and tries to be like Ambrosch, she admits, "If I live here [with the Burdens], like you, that is different. Things will be easy for you. But they will be hard for us" (140). This reflection ends the first book on a quiet note after its dramatic finale, a summer electric storm with lightning flashes and loud, metallic thunder. Here is another Virgilian touch, the mighty summer storm in the middle of georgic 1:

> Down headlong falls the sky
> In sheets; the glad fruits of the oxen's labours
> Are washed away . . .
> . . . .
> The Father himself in the midmost night of cloud
> Wields thunderbolts amain. The mighty earth
> Quakes at the shock.
>
> (324–31)

In Jim's description of the storm, "All the west was luminous and clear. . . . One black cloud . . . drifted out into the clear space unattended, and kept moving westward" (139). These details are ambiguous, perhaps anticipating Ántonia's final triumph and his own disappointments; or perhaps the cloud suggests her ruin, or the sexual difficulties and social prejudices dramatized in the second book.

BOOK 2, "THE HIRED GIRLS"

Like book 1 this book records initiation and exploration adventures, but in reference to sex and social conditions rather than space and landscape. Two years pass between the books, and Jim moves to the little town of Black Hawk for the second installment of his memoir. This town, "a clean, well-planted" place (145), becomes a way station on his journey through the stages of civilization. As Bernice Slote has commented, "the order of the book takes us from the kind of country Willa Cather first knew in Nebraska of the 1880s—unsettled, young, rough . . . , to the first small communities . . . , to cities and universities; and while there, through the mind and imagination, to the world of ideas and the arts, of history alive." One indication of this development is the introduction of music and dance; harmonica tunes, cowboy songs, and the unaccompanied funeral hymn are now replaced by piano playing at the Harlings', the black pianist at the hotel, and the orchestra at the dancing tent—indeed, dancing weaves itself through the book in a manner reminiscent of Bruegel's "Wedding Dance in the Open Air."

Transition to Town The transition to town life is not necessarily a positive development. Jim soon learns to "fight, play 'keeps,' tease the little girls, and use forbidden words . . ." (145). Settled into a fancy house in town with trumpet-blowing cherubs on the parlor ceiling, he wants to share his experiences with Ántonia, who enters in the third chapter (her entrance point in the first book) as the hired girl of the Harling family, whose members Jim introduces in a series of excellent thumbnail sketches—the paragraph on Mrs. Harling, for example, is worthy of Chaucer in its graphic rendering of character. His literary achievements are not always on such a high level, however, and he proceeds to reveal a taste for sentimental melodrama when describing how his grandfather and Frances Harling often "put their wits together to rescue some unfortunate farmer from the clutches of Wick Cutter, the Black Hawk money-lender" (150). (Jim's increasing compulsion to use various literary methods rather indiscriminately to exaggerate or minimize his experiences should warn us against accepting at face value everything he tells us.) The Harlings and Burdens also rescue Ántonia from the clutches of ambitious Ambrosch, who has taken to hiring her out as a field worker. The earth goddess is summarily brought to town and put into shoes and stockings, although she preserves her "fine brown legs and arms, and splendid colour in her cheeks—like those big dark red plums" (153). The girl proves successful at the Harlings'; however, there are several indications in these otherwise jolly opening chapters of her eventual ruin. The evil Wick Cutter will help make prophetic her brother's complaint that they are dressing her up to "make a fool out of her" (152), and what Jim describes as Mr. Harling's hauteur and arrogance will drive her into Cutter's clutches. Most of all, she will be done in by her weakness for the kind of blind devotion she exhibits when she pads in her carpet slippers after Charley Harling. As she confesses at the end, "The trouble with me was . . . I never could believe harm of anybody I loved" (344).

Ántonia's foil, Lena Lingard, now enters to highlight the sexual dependence, maternal tendencies, and domestic abilities of the Ántonia Jim creates for us. Lena is a girl with a "reputation" for making men crazy, yet she is worldly-wise enough to avoid entrapment by them. Ántonia is hesitant about welcoming this "talked about" friend at the Harlings' and responds with a cold, lace-curtain propriety that makes her own eventual ruin all the more ironic. Lena's white skin, straying, soft violet eyes, and love for clothes are in dramatic contrast to the brown eyes and hair and indifference to clothes of her counterpart. Attracted to Lena in the sexual way he cannot be to Ántonia, Jim distinguishes her from other country girls: "I was astonished at her soft voice and easy, gentle ways. The girls out there usually got rough and mannish after they went to herding" (165). Lena's laughter during the retrospective melodrama when crazy Mary Benson threatens to trim her with a corn knife for tempting her husband associates her with Venus. She vehemently rejects farm life, marriage, and motherhood, yet reveals a tender, maternal side during her shopping expedition with her brother Chris. Lena's love for her mother matches Ántonia's love for her father, and both girls possess a strong sense of family. The information we get on the Lingard family and the Benson marriage, and the chilling effect of Mr. Harling on his family contribute to the developing theme that marriage is less than an ideal institution.

Winter Pictures As in the first book, Jim uses the cycle of seasons as a splicing device. The two chapters devoted to winter in town (6 and 7) frame pictures comparable to those framed in book 1. Jim introduces the season by associating defoliation with truth exposed through summer's attempts to obscure it: "This is reality, whether you like it or not," sings the bitter wind. "All those frivolities of summer, the light and shadow, the living mask of green that trembled over everything, they were lies, and this is what was underneath. This is the truth" (173). The purgatorial theme from the earlier book is reintroduced in the comment that "It was as if we were being punished for loving the loveliness of summer." The pictures immediately following, of despair, handicap, and emotional transference, suggest the harsh realities beneath both Jim's apparently straightforward recollection of his childhood and his summer visit to the middle-aged Ántonia in book 5.

To frame the first picture darkness and cold are stressed, and the consequent hunger for color and heat. The image of children clustered before the lighted painted window of the Methodist church recalls the poignant fascination of Paul in Cather's short story "Paul's Case" as he watched through the drizzle the lighted windows of Pittsburgh's Schenley Hotel. The atmosphere and activities in the Harling house—warmth, sweet smells, candy-making, dancing, and tellings stories—are as vivid amid the bleakness as the "crude reds and greens and blues of that coloured glass" (174), and as satisfying to winter hunger. Ántonia provides the picture for this winter frame. In contrast to winter, in it "The sun was so hot like it was going to burn the world up" during threshing time, when "chaff . . . gets down your neck and sticks . . . something awful" in the heat (177–78). Perhaps a sacrificial victim to ensure the fruitfulness of the next year's crops, the tramp who throws himself into the threshing machine parallels Shimerda as a suicide, but amid burning brightness rather than stiffening cold. Also, as a recollection of past events, the story parallels the celebration of Christmas on the prairie, but it is of death and despair rather than birth and hope. At its conclusion, Mrs. Harling changes the tone by drawing attention to nice weather and the odor of taffy, and Jim focuses a comparison of Ántonia and her mistress around their hearty, independent natures and relish of life.

References to "shrunken and pinched" life, "frozen down to the bare stalk" (181), bring us back to winter as Jim prepares a frame for the story of a man who, like Mr. Shimerda, is a musician, the blind pianist Samson d'Arnault. The setting for his performance is the Boys' Home Hotel, operated by the Gardeners, whose marriage provides Jim with a foil for the Harling marriage. Like Mr. Harling, Mrs. Gardener is the inhibiting factor in this relationship, although her husband hardly corresponds to the energetic Mrs. Harling. The description of Blind d'Arnault, appropriately racist and sentimental, suggests the lack of objectivity built into Jim's narrative. He rhapsodizes over the "amiable Negro voice" and the "happiest face I had seen since I left Virginia," and he refers to "My Old Kentucky Home" as a "Negro melody" (184–85); more pointedly, he describes "the Negro head" as "almost no head at all; nothing behind the ears but folds of neck under close-clipped wool" (Jim's description in book 5 of the head of Ántonia's violin-playing son Leo is curiously similar [348]), and concludes: "To hear him, to watch him, was to see a Negro enjoying himself as only a Negro can" (189). The blind man's story, like the tramp's, is set in warmth and in the past, on a plantation "in the Far South" (185). As the story of a misfit it is linked to the tramp's, a connection underscored by references in both to chicken bones: other children had tried to get the blind child's "chicken-bone away from him" (185), and "the wish bone of a chicken wrapped up in a piece of paper" (179) was found in the tramp's pocket.

The pianist's story also reflects Jim Burden's as a paradigm of suppression and rechanneling. Piano playing, like Jim's writing, becomes therapeutic as a means of self-completion. Just as Jim creates in his memoir the maternal heroine he needs to share with him "the precious, the incommunicable past" (372) that completes him, d'Arnault pursued the seductive song of the piano and "coupled himself to [the instrument], as if he knew it was to piece him out and make a whole creature of him" (188). The piano becomes, in effect, his woman: "He touched it softly, and it answered softly, kindly. He shivered and stood still. Then he began to feel it all over, ran his fingertips along the slippery sides, embraced the carved legs. . . . He went back to its mouth, began at one end of the keyboard and felt his way down to mellow thunder, as far as he could go" (187). The art produced, like Jim's, is hardly professional: "As piano-playing, it was perhaps abominable, but as music it was something real . . ." (189). At the conclusion of the performance and dance at the Boys' Home, the frame closes with a reminder of winter; Jim and Ántonia linger at the Harlings' gate, "whispering in the cold until the restlessness [is] slowly chilled out of [them]" (192).

Disruptions of Venus With the coming of spring and summer in the next chapters (8 to 12) there is a return to the Genesis theme of lapse from innocence. In spring the children play in the Harling garden, "never happier, . . . more contented and secure. . . . I could hear Tony singing in the garden rows. After the apple and cherry trees broke into bloom, we ran about under them, hunting for new nests . . . , throwing clods at each other, and playing hide-and-seek . . ." (193). But all of this changes—sex enters the garden. It becomes the season for growing up, "the summer which was to change everything." As Virgil says of the blinding effects of Venus;

> Indeed all species in the world, of men,
> Wild beasts and fish, cattle and coloured birds
> Rush madly into the furnace: love is common
> To all.
>
> (3:242–45)

A traveling dancing pavilion becomes the arena for sexual display and social leveling. The dancing school itself, attended by girls in white dresses and boys in round-collared shirts, offers no threat, but there is a seductive element in the freedom of movement of the hired, country girls in their cheap finery. The dances, operated by an Italian family, the Vannis, cultural outsiders like the Irish traveling salesmen Kirkpatrick and O'Reilly, who encourage dancing at the Boys' Home over the protests of Johnnie Gardener, disrupt the order of the fundamentalist Protestant town. Lena, Tiny Soderball, the Danish laundry girls, even Ántonia develop the reputation of the Bohemian Marys "as dangerous as high explosives" (204).

Jim now explores the rigid class structure of Black Hawk, the distinction made between Pennsylvania or Virginia people, or successful Minnesota Scandinavians like Mr. Harling, and foreigners—especially those on farms rather than running businesses in town. Jim differentiates between the foreign girls who "had grown up in the first bitter-hard times, and had got little schooling" (198), and the privileged girls in his school, whom he remembers as bodiless, "cut off below the shoulders, like cherubs, by the ink-smeared tops of the high desks . . ." (199). There was adventure in dancing with the foreign girls, in sultry waltzes with Lena and in breathless "schottisches" with Ántonia. But when one danced with the daughters of respected families, "their bodies never moved inside their clothes; their muscles seemed to ask but one thing—not to be disturbed" (199). Jim's preference for the former is comparable to Virgil's singling out the hardy dams in the *Georgics* as most appropriate for purposes of breeding. Town boys failed to appreciate the social quality of some of the hired girls, made no distinctions between those who came from cultivated families in the Old World and those of lower classes, and dismissed them all as ignorant foreigners deficient in English. They were enticed sexually by them, however, and let their eyes follow Lena's undulating walk or Tiny's short skirt and striped stockings. When everybody got mixed up at the Vannis' dances ("anyone could dance who paid his money" [197]), the country girls became a menace to the social order: "their beauty shone out too boldly against a conventional background" (201).

In his indictment of Black Hawk's "white-handed, high-collared clerks and book-keepers" (204), Jim tells the story of Sylvester Lovett, a cashier in his family's bank, who was, like Ole Benson, infatuated with Lena and danced with her every Saturday night. "In my ingenuousness," confesses Jim, "I hoped that Sylvester would marry Lena, and thus give all the country girls a better position in the town (203–4). But to "escape from his predicament [Sylvester] ran away with a widow six years older than himself, who owned a half-section" (204). Jim concludes that "anxious mothers need have felt no alarm. They mistook the mettle of their sons. The respect for respectability was stronger than any desire in Black Hawk youth" (201–2). There is significant irony here, perhaps the result of Jim's confessed ingenuousness, for when his grandmother gets upset at his dancing, he admits that "Disapprobation hurt me . . . even that of people I did not admire" (228). An inability to see clearly, which should affect our estimate of him and his beloved girls, characterizes the writer of these pages, who includes a comment by Frances Harling important for gauging the veracity of his narrative: "I expect I know the country girls better than you do. You always put a kind of glamour over them. The trouble with you, Jim, is that you're romantic" (229).

Paralleling this inability to see clearly is Jim's dilemma of sexual response. His feelings for Lena, evident in his descriptions of her, are blatantly sexual. He appreciates her enticing indolence, the soft touch of her fingers on his shoulder, her sleepy eyes, her perfume-laden sighs. Like Venus, she constantly smiles, and waltzing with her "was like coming in with the tide" (222). He admits kissing Lena on the mouth when Ántonia rejects this kind of kiss and threatens to tell his grandmother on him. He would like to feel about Ántonia as he does about Lena, but Ántonia resists his futile efforts in this direction. His dancing with Ántonia is as romantic as an athletic event—"she had so much spring and variety, and was always putting in new steps and slides" (223). The dreams he has about these girls clarify his responses and how they run counter to his intentions. He dreams of sliding down straw-stacks with Ántonia out in the country, but Lena appears in his dreams as a fertility goddess with a curved reaping hook and a rosy glow about her, who approaches his supine figure in a harvest field and threatens to kiss him as much as she likes. He caps these descriptions with a confession of his frustration: "I used to wish I could have this flattering dream about Ántonia, but I never did" (226).

Ántonia, true to the lace-curtain respectability she displayed when Lena appeared at the Harlings', forces his conformity to the conventional route pursued by ambitious young men from respectable families, like Charley Harling (now at Annapolis). "You're going away to school and make something of yourself," she admonishes, like a mother or big sister, after Jim tries to kiss her. "I'm just awful proud of you. You won't go and get mixed up with the Swedes, will you?" (224). Her obvious warning against girls of her own set, who are sexually free and "can't help it" (225), makes her an ironic defender of the intolerance of the town, a girl who knows her place. She becomes a factor in Jim's being shut out of Black Hawk's few places of pleasure. His oft-quoted diatribe against the town (219–20) (frequently interpreted as Cather's own revolt-from-the-village sentiments) for bridling every natural appetite and every individual taste under the tyranny of caution, is partially motivated by confusion, self pity, and displeasure with himself.

As an added irony, Ántonia herself by this time has been expelled from the garden where the children innocently played. The Vannis' dances are the occasion of this change, and Jim's comment about it has definite biblical overtones: "Hitherto she had been looked upon more as a ward of the Harlings than as one of the 'hired girls.' She had lived in their house and yard and garden; her thoughts never seemed to stray outside that little kingdom. But after the tent came to town she began to go about with Tiny and Lena and their friends" (204–5). She begins to live to dance, becomes irresponsible at her job, breaks dishes, is followed by young men to the Harling back porch, and incurs the wrath of Mr. Harling. Confronted with his ultimatum to stop going to the dances or leave his house, she chooses the latter and takes a job with the Cutters. She admits to Mrs. Harling that she has changed but excuses herself by insisting that a girl like her "has to take her good times when she can. Maybe there won't be any tent next year. I guess I want to have my fling, like the other girls" (208). Her employment by Wick Cutter, the money lender associated with the snake in book 1 and described as a snake during his attempt to rape Ántonia, suggests her going to the devil. "After Ántonia went to live with the Cutters," writes Jim, "she seemed to care about nothing but picnics and parties and having a good time" (214).

The portrait of the Cutters Jim now introduces is the most grotesque in his gallery of marriages; in a sterile relationship based on hate, the Cutters "seemed to find their relations to each other interesting and stimulating . . ." (213). As befitting the Father of Lies, Cutter contributes regularly to the Protestant churches, spouts moral maxims, quotes "Poor Richard," and impregnates his hired girls; also, he lives in a fussy, white house and presents to the public a meticulous, factory-made countenance. Jim's obvious association of sex with evil does more than reveal a puritan with a talent for stock villains; it reveals Jim's own sexual frustration and reminds us of his failed marriage. After she goes to live at the Cutters', Ántonia meets the architect of her ruin, the passenger conductor Larry Donovan, "a kind of professional ladies' man" (223). Her ruin, which Jim knows about as he writes his account, merely confirms his own warped attitudes toward sex.

Consequences The final three chapters of this book (13 to 15) complete its major themes and end on a strangely unsettling note. In the first, Jim's sneaking off to the Firemen's Hall dances against the wishes of his grandmother is discovered, and he promises to stay home. His response to his grandmother's complaint that talk has it that he is growing up a bad boy is a brave "I don't care what they say about me" (227), which he contradicts a few lines later. More significant perhaps is his reading Latin in the evenings to prepare to go away to college, from which point we might trace his escape from life and into letters. In the process of tidying up at high school and giving a successful commencement oration, he pleases Mrs. Harling, who forgives him for taking Ántonia's part in her husband's dispute with the girl, and he makes Ántonia proud of him. His scene with her, Lena, and Anna Hansen—three figures in white—is poignant because it indicates these girls' respect for the education that circumstances prevent them from having and because it recalls the tragic figure of Mr. Shimerda, to whom Jim dedicated his speech.

The central chapter of the three is one of the most important in Cather. It begins with a reference to reading Virgil, mentions the *Aeneid,* and ends with the famous plow passage recalling the celebration of the plow in *Georgics.* During the one holiday of his last summer in Black Hawk, Jim goes to the river for a final get-together with his beloved hired girls. He catalogs the many-colored fields on the way to meet them, comparing the gaillardia to the velvety red in Bokhara carpets, lounges and swims in the river, and listens to the buzz of the wild bees, which continues after he joins Ántonia beneath the flowering elders in a reminiscence of her father. She tells him of the circumstances of her parents' marriage, yet another unhappy, uneven, discouraging relationship. They are interrupted in their innocent intimacy by mocking, panting Lena, the seductress, who charges the atmosphere with energy. Then Jim and the hired girls picnic overlooking the rolling country, and the girls point in the direction of their families' farms and tell of the trials of farm-work and too many children, of disappointments and hopes for the future—Anna, for example, would have liked to teach school, and Lena intends to go into business for herself. Jim tells them of the defeated expectations of Spanish explorer Coronado, who traveled to these plains in his search for the Seven Golden Cities but died in the wilderness, like Mr. Shimerda, of a broken heart. There is talk of a Spanish sword turned up by a plow in Nebraska and then, in a passage worthy of a luminist painter, Jim describes the fiery setting sun glittering over grass, trees, and river, and magnifying a distant plow in the field into something "heroic in size, a picture writing on the sun": "it stood out against the sun, was exactly contained within the circle of the disk; the handles, the tongue, the share—black against the molten red" (245). This image recalls the beginning section of *Georgics,* where almost twenty lines are devoted to a description of the handles, the share, and the beam of the plow (1:160–77). Virgil closes this first georgic with a war and peace theme, lamenting the war-torn country, where pruning hooks are straightened into swords, heralding the final triumph of the plow, when battlefields will become wheat fields, and anticipating Cather's Nebraska farmer turning up the Spanish sword:

> Surely the time will come when in these regions
> The farmer heaving the soil with his curved plough
> Will come on spears all eaten up with rust
> Or strike with his heavy hoe on hollow helmets,
> And gape at the huge bones in the upturned graves.
>   (1:493–97)

Both passages, Jim's and Virgil's, recall Isaiah's hopeful prophecy of the prosperity of new countries: "He will wield authority over the peoples; these will hammer their swords into plowshares, and spears into sickles. Nation will not lift sword against nation, there will be no more training for war" (2:4). Since Jim's writing of his memoir seems to correspond in time with Cather's writing of *My Ántonia* (1916–18), the last stages of World War I, he probably, like Cather and Virgil, is preoccupied with the theme of war and peace, which might partially explain his obvious emptiness and his need to come home to himself, as expressed in the novel's final paragraph.

The last chapter of "The Hired Girls" contains the upshot of Ántonia's defection to the Cutters. To infuriate his wife even more than usual Cutter puts her on a train for Kansas City and then himself returns to Black Hawk from Omaha with the intention of raping Ántonia. However, Jim has taken Ántonia's place and is the one who must struggle with the "hissing and chuckling" (248) madman in a scene paralleling the struggle with the hideous snake in book 1. It is interesting to compare Jim's queasiness in both these scenes, and his bitterness at Ántonia for involving him in them. The choice of this chapter for an ending is curious and strategic—the plow against the sun would be a happier and more conventional finale, somewhat like the summer storm at the end of "The Shimerdas." What begins on a bucolic note of happy children in a garden ends with the image of a badly disfigured face, room torn to chaos, trampled clothing, anger, and resentment.

Book 3, "Lena Lingard"

This short strategic book, mentioned earlier as the filter from which the entire text should be reviewed, is the climax, the turning point of Jim Burden's story. It opens in Lincoln, where he is attending the new University of Nebraska, the third stage in his journey from country to village to small prairie city, an eastward movement that will take him to Harvard, Europe, and then New York City, where he is living when he composes his memoir.

Crisis An important new influence on Jim is the displaced New England intellectual Gaston Cleric, whose somewhat unusual befriending of the raw Black Hawk freshman is looked back upon by him as a "time of mental awakening . . . one of the happiest [times] in my life" (257). Jim and Cleric play tennis, read, and take long walks together, and among his classmates he "alone knew Cleric intimately enough" to guess his feelings for his "particular rocky strip of New England coast" (265). This bachelor makes the classics alive for Jim, creates a romantic and adventurous world in tension with "the streets of Lincoln, which were almost as quiet and oppressively domestic as those of Black Hawk" (260). If one recalls the bitter tone and imagery of Jim's condemnation of his village and juxtaposes them with his fond imaginings of Cleric's solitary day among the temples in southern Italy, and memories of his lingering over Benedictine and fancy cigarettes in Jim's study, Jim's isolating and romantic tendencies become obvious and his studies in Virgil and Dante under Cleric's direction somewhat solipsistic. Incapable of being a scholar because he could never "lose" himself for long "among impersonal things" (262), Jim begins to view the people and places of his past through the medium of his reading. "They stood out strengthened and simplified now," he says, "like the image of the plough against the sun" (262). The recollection of the plow here is a reminder that its "heroic" proportions in "the horizontal light" (245) depend upon perception and are a matter of approaching reality in a certain light, that Jim's perception rescues the people and places of his childhood from their *reality* as it rescues the "forgotten plough" from "its own littleness . . . on the prairie" (245). These people and places are so much "alive" in him that he "scarcely stopped to wonder whether they were alive anywhere else, or how" (262).

Jim's conflict is twofold, partly of commitment and partly of perception. The latter is between his awareness of things as they are, as far as that is possible, and his compulsion to color them out of proportion, what he calls strengthening and simplifying them. His description of the young university lifting its head from the prairie (258) is, like many in the novel, in the realistic tradition, but when he describes his preparations for studying on the evening during the March thaw when Lena visits him, the result is purpled with painterly and literary images as well as extravagant language and presented in breathless, rhythmic phrases alternating with longer clauses:

> On the edge of the prairie, where the sun had gone down, the sky was turquoise blue, like a lake, with gold light throbbing in it. Higher up, in the utter clarity of the western slope, the evening star hung like a lamp suspended by silver chains—like the lamp engraved upon the title-page of old Latin texts, which is always appearing in new heavens, and waking new desires in men. It reminded me, at any rate, to shut my window and light my wick in answer. I did so regretfully, and the dim objects in the room emerged

from the shadows and took their place about me with the helpful-
ness which custom breeds. (263)

Such self-conscious composing is an increasing ingredient in the last
two books, especially when Jim bids good-bye to Ántonia in the midst
of her ruin, and when he returns two decades later to strengthen and
simplify her as a founder of early races.

In the romanticized setting of his study Jim contemplates two passages from Virgil's *Georgics*. The first, the "melancholy reflection that,
in the lives of mortals, the best days are the first to flee" (Cather, 263;
Virgil, 3:67–69), refers in the original to sturdy dams worn out in their
prime through repeated breeding and too weakened to plow—the implication being that the best days for Jim and for a sturdy breeder like
Ántonia were those before puberty. The second passage is connected
to Jim's developing penchant to view his past aesthetically. In it Virgil's
intention is to choose humble country activities as his unhackneyed
theme and "by mastery of words / To invest such humble things with
dignity" (3:290–91); he accordingly calls upon the deities Pales and
Apollo to help him

> be first, if life is granted me,
> To lead in triumph from Greek Helicon
> To my native land the Muses. I will be first
> To bring you, Mantua, Idumaean palms,
> And in green meadows raise a marble temple
> Beside the water where the Mincius,
> Embroidering his banks with tender rushes,
> In sweeping loops meanders.
>
> (3:9–16)

Jim's obvious identification with this boast or intention, mixed up as
it is with reflections on his teacher Cleric, is now "disturbed" (265),
as was his tête-è-tête with Ántonia at the picnic, by the entrance of
Lena. Even in tailored black she is the seductress, removing her jacket,
exposing her "flimsy silk" blouse (266), slipping comfortably into
Jim's surroundings and, her elbows on the table, turning her soft cheek

cheek to him and whispering, "come and see me sometimes" (270). This intrusion threatens the solipsistic bachelor life Jim shares with Cleric and emphasizes the second part of Jim's conflict, commitment. However, Jim will successfully transform Lena, through a kind of literary gymnastics, to one of the figures of his manipulated past. Superimposing the Virgilian epigraph "*Optima dies ... prima fugit*" beneath his dream image of her anticipates his resolution of this conflict.

At this point Dumas's play *La Dame aux Camelias* is introduced as a clue to Jim's and Lena's situations and as a means of emotional transference for Jim. Certain aspects of Lena's situation parallel Marguerite Gautier's. Lena keeps a little parlor, albeit stiff and with hard horsehair furniture, in which she receives her men friends; she is doted on by old Colonel Raleigh, who gives her gifts, and is protected by a jealous Polish violinist. There are strong suggestions that she has an affair with Jim, although his comments both deny and affirm this. They frequently breakfast together, and he notes that "Lena was never so pretty as in the morning; she wakened fresh with the world every day, and her eyes had a deeper colour then, like the blue flowers that are never so blue as when they first open. I could sit idle all through a Sunday morning and look at her" (281–82). But Jim makes clear to the suspicious Pole that he is not compromising her (286–87). Lena's sincere interest in Jim parallels Marguerite's in Armand Duval, but unlike Camille, Lena pursues rather than is pursued by her young lover. Like Camille, she is associated with flowers, but the language of her flowers indicates that she is less cunning about her lover. For example, where Marguerite refuses roses (*love*) and white lilacs (*youthful innocence*) at the beginning of the play, Lena presents herself to Jim wearing forget-me-nots (*true love*) and is seen carrying home jonquils (*I desire a return of affection*), although these are somewhat undercut by the hyacinth plants (*sport, game, play*) she sometimes carries to confirm her reputation as a flirt. We must consider Lena serious about Jim and not completely honest about her feelings when she sends him away at last with a "soft, slow, renunciatory kiss" (293). Marguerite, at the request of Armand's father and to protect the young man's future career and the reputation of his distinguished family, turns Armand away, falsely insisting she does not love him. This suggests that Lena might have been appealed to in behalf of Jim when Cleric discovered him "drifting" with this "perfectly irresponsible" Norwegian (289). When Jim arrives at Lena's to break the news that he is leaving Lincoln to continue his studies at Harvard, she anticipates his announcement with a rejection of marriage and home life incompletely sincere, which makes it easier for him when he drops down beside her, having "forgotten all [his] reasonable explanations" (293), to put an end to the affair. One recalls Marguerite's line to her confidante Nichette near the beginning of act 3: "If I wished it Armand would marry me tomorrow, but I love him far too well to ask such a thing."

Jim's description of the performance of Dumas's play is important not only because it reflects his and Lena's situations by concentrating on Marguerite's painful acquiescence to the request of the elder Duval that she renounce his son, but because it demonstrates Jim's ability to make over reality for his convenience and to transfer his emotions from life to art. He describes the actress as "already old, with a ravaged countenance and a physique curiously hard and stiff. . . . But what would it matter? I believed devoutly in her power to fascinate [Armand], in her dazzling loveliness. I believed her young, ardent, reckless, disillusioned, under sentence, feverish, avid of pleasure" (274). This is a rehearsal for the final book, for his making Ántonia, "a battered woman now," into someone who "fires the imagination, could still stop one's breath . . ." (353). Confusion between life and art is evident in Jim's wanting "to cross the footlights and help the slim-waisted Armand . . . convince her that there was still loyalty and devotion in the world" (274). However, during Marguerite's scene with the elder Duval, Jim "sat helpless to prevent the closing of that idyllic love" (275), a helplessness evident later when he drops beside Lena to end their affair. At the tragic close of the play he "wept unrestrainedly" (277), but he closes his affair with Lena abruptly and without emotion, visits his grandparents in Black Hawk and his relatives in Virginia, and is off to Harvard.

His experience with Lena amounts to a magnified version of Sylvester Lovett's, who like Jim drifted with her and lost interest in his work. But Jim did not cure himself by running away with a widow; he ran away with Cleric to Harvard and pursued the route of success charted out for him by Ántonia, who wanted him to achieve great things and avoid "nonsense" with Lena (224). So the crisis is resolved, Jim remaining true to the destiny of privileged old stock Americans and recalling the appeal of M. Duval to the courtesan in the third act: "You and my son have two very different roads to follow; chance has brought them together for a moment. You have been happy for three months; do not sully that happiness; keep the memory of it always in your heart."

Book 4, "The Pioneer Woman's Story"

This book begins somewhat prosaically, chapters 1 and 2 taking up Jim's story two years after he "solved" his relationship with Lena, recording his visit to his grandparents in Black Hawk before returning to Harvard Law School to prepare for a career with the railroads. The title chapter (3) is the tale of Ántonia's ruin told by pioneer woman Widow Steavens, and the final chapter (4) ends in a rhapsody to childhood friendship and archetypal woman, Jim's solution to his relationship with Ántonia.

Departure When Jim first returns to Black Hawk, "Everything seemed as it used to be" (297) except for Ántonia's fall. He admits that at first he tried "to shut Ántonia out of my mind. I was bitterly disappointed in her. I could not forgive her for becoming an object of pity, while Lena Lingard, for whom people had always foretold trouble, was now the leading dressmaker of Lincoln, much respected in Black Hawk" (298). His strategy was to compare Ántonia with girls he had considered less worthy, and in what at first may seem a digression he inserts here the success story of Tiny Soderball, who had speculated in the Klondike and become so rich in gold "that nothing interested her much . . . but making money" (301). Tiny's story is intertwined with Lena's when the two spinsters share life together in San Francisco and ends on the sour note that Tiny became "like someone in whom the faculty of becoming interested is worn out" (302).

Thus Jim actually distinguishes Ántonia, whose final success in his eyes will be as golden spiritually as Tiny's is materially, and whose extraordinary interest in all living things is perpetual. Seeing a crayoned photograph of her illegitimate daughter in Black Hawk softens his bitterness, for he recognizes that "another girl would have kept her baby out of sight . . ." (303). Overcoming what is left of his resentment toward railroad conductor Larry Donovan by demolishing him as vain and worthless, a worse cad even than Sylvester Lovett, the bank clerk who had toyed with Lena, Jim goes to Mrs. Steavens to hear a story that conveniently for him resembles in many aspects the Nativity story he celebrated years before when he decorated Jake's Christmas tree with Otto's creche cutouts. Like an evangelist, Jim records what he hears about Ántonia, adding the widow's eyewitness account to information collected from Mrs. Harling, her daughter Frances, and the town photographer. He gives the old woman's account verbatim, including in it her asides and complaints of ailments. She tells of Ántonia's excitement at the prospect of marriage, gives details about the assembling of the dowry, describes her departure to Denver and then her abandonment and return in shame to Black Hawk—penniless, pregnant, and unmarried—and to the comfort of the prairie. When Ántonia confessed to her, the widow exclaims, "I sat right down on that bank beside her and made lament" (313), echoing Psalm 137 (Ballad of the Exiles): "Beside the streams of Babylon we sat and wept at the memory of Zion. . . ." She marvels at Ántonia's calmness, perseverance, humility, and then describes her dark period of hard work in the fields, ulcerated teeth, and exposure to Ambrosch's bitterness. There is a strong suggestion of justice in this, that the girl suffered for her sin: "She was so crushed and quiet," continues the widow, "that nobody seemed to want to humble her" (314). Finally, on a snowy day near Christmas she returned with the cattle she was shepherding, "went into the house, into her room behind the kitchen, and . . . without calling to anybody, without a groan . . . she lay down on the bed and bore her child" (316). There are echoes in this story of Matthew and Luke: of Mary's shame in being discovered with child, Joseph's attempt to put her away (Matt. 1:18–20), Mary's humility (Luke 1: 46–48), of the humble stable birth when another "natural born" mother "wrapped [her child] in swaddling clothes, and laid him in a manger" (Luke 2:17). The suggestion, especially in light of the fruit-cave scene in the last book, is that Ántonia's girl baby, like Mary's male one, is the child of some universal force, that its paternity is connected with the spirit of the land to which its mother surrendered in her sorrow. Even when Ántonia came "in from the fields" during her pregnancy, says the widow, she "talked about the grain and the weather as if she'd never had another interest . . ." (314). Such intimacy with nature continues in the last chapter (4), where Ántonia tells Jim directly that she would "be miserable in a city. I'd die of lonesomeness. I like to be where I know every stack and tree, and where all the ground is friendly. I want to live and die here" (320).

This final chapter clearly illustrates the effect of Jim's aesthetic perception of experience, not only in retrospect (as with events before the third book) but initially. Taking his clues from Mrs. Steavens's "scriptural" account, Jim meets Ántonia in the fields "like the people in the old song, in silence, if not in tears" (319), and walks with her to her father's grave to discuss their lives and the future. Unashamed, the future Harvard lawyer utters at this point his famous conditional proposal to his unwed mother friend—a WASP tribute to a Bohunk: "I'd have liked to have you for a sweetheart, or a wife, or my mother or my sister—anything that a woman can be to a man" (321). He is accepting here, in his own way, the union symbolized by the little silver ring she had offered him early in the first book. But he restricts his possession of her to the imaginative realm, where she can be refined and idealized, after he views her in the sunset light so precious to painters for clothing the prosaic with magic. His poetic arousal in this instance substitutes for the sexual failure in his relationship with her: "In that singular light every little tree and shock of wheat, every sunflower stalk and clump of snow-on-the-mountain, drew itself up high and pointed; the very clods and furrows in the fields seemed to stand up sharply" (322). As the "golden globe" sun and silver and rose "ghost moon" confront "each other across the level land" (321–22), we are reminded again of divine maternity, for both celestial bodies appear in Marian iconography based on Revelation 12:1: "Now a great sign appeared in heaven: a woman, adorned with the sun, standing on the moon, and with twelve stars on her head for a crown." We are reminded also of the sky–earth, male–female counterpoise in the early ring scene and can speculate on the sun and moon as symbols of male and female, respectively, for Ántonia like the moon basks in Jim's imaginative light—Jim has been associated with the sky and she with the illumined earth. The face Jim deciphers in the darkening light, "the closest, realist face, under all the shadows of women's faces," he determines "always to carry with [him] . . . at the very bottom of [his] memory" (322).

Having devised an imaginative solution to a relationship characterized by sexual failure and now by social disgrace, as he had to a relationship in Lincoln characterized by career-threatening sexual response, Jim departs, promising to return. In the process he resurrects the childhood image of his and Ántonia's shadows moving across the grass, which looks backward to the first book, where Ántonia revived the freezing insect and he noticed "two long black shadows" (40) sometimes flitting before them, sometimes following after.

BOOK 5, "CUZAK'S BOYS"

The three chapters in this book emphasize overlapping themes of resurrection or restoration, fecundity and marriage, and return. Jim introduces the last of these with the comment that "life intervened, and it was twenty years before I kept my promise" to return to Ántonia (327). The "life" he refers to is, according to the introduction, his successful and wandering career as "legal counsel for one of the great Western railways" and his failed and childless marriage to a seemingly unimpressionable, unenthusiastic patroness of the arts, who lives her own life and is irritated by her husband's "quiet tastes." Jim's return is obviously connected to a mid-life crisis, a theme handled in most Cather novels, which involves reflections on and/or return to youth or childhood. In *My Ántonia* the return is to some extent physical, an actual return to what Jim feels is his "road of Destiny," that rough road over the prairie he traveled with Ántonia when he was ten years old. Definitely therapeutic, the return is a question of his own survival, although his text is washed of such urgency. He does confess to the importance of the image of Ántonia he has carried with him all these years, that he fears (owing to the biased reports of materialistic Tiny) finding her "aged and broken": "In the course of twenty crowded years one parts with many illusions. I did not wish to lose the early ones" (328). Obviously he hesitates to have his image of Ántonia join the ruined ones of his wife and himself. Lena comes to the rescue, as she had in the third book, challenging him to face reality: "You really ought to go, Jim. It would be such a satisfaction to her. . . . Tony has nice children—ten or eleven of them by this time, I guess. . . . She'd love to show them to you" (328–29).

Return Jim's confrontation with his now life-battered ideal occurs one summer's end (the time of year when his memoir begins). As he approaches her farm he discovers two of her boys bending over a dead dog, an image of death that prepares us for the explosion of life from the fruit cave in a later scene. His first view of his old friend is "a shock, of course" (331), but by focusing on Ántonia's eyes rather than her flat chest, grizzled hair, and almost toothless mouth, he manages to preserve his illusion: "As I confronted her, the changes grew less apparent to me, her identity stronger. She was there, in the full vigour of her personality, battered but not diminished, looking at me, speaking to me in the husky, breathy voice I remembered so well" (331–32). Overcoming this initial hurdle, Jim manages to resurrect the dead past through Ántonia's accomplishment. Her children, for example, bear the names of her brother and sister, the Harling children, and other friends, thereby restoring them all to childhood. Her father lives again in Easter-baby Leo, the lamb-like son with the lion's name who plays old Shimerda's violin. The climactic image of children bursting from the fruit cave fuses several of the novel's thematic patterns—Ántonia as earth mother, metaphysical paternity, Christmas, and resurrection or rebirth after death. After leaving the cave with Ántonia, Jim looks back on her brood: "they all came running up the steps together, big and little, tow heads and gold heads and brown, and flashing little naked legs; a veritable explosion of life out of the dark cave into the sunlight" (338–39). Recalling old Shimerda's grotesque corpse, we are reminded of the resurrection image in Whitman's "Song of Myself": "the grave of rock multiplies what has been confided to it, or to any graves, / Corpses rise, gashes heal, fastenings roll from me" (968–69). But this is more than the resurrection of a family or of childhood; superimposed upon that is the birth of a generation of new people in a new country. Jim caps the first chapter with another purple rhapsody on his friend: "She lent herself to immemorial human attitudes . . . , universal and true . . . ; [she] still had that something which fires the imagination, . . . revealed the meaning in common things, . . . [made] you feel the goodness of planting and tending and harvesting at last. . . . It was no wonder that her sons stood tall and straight. She was a rich mine of life, like the founders of early races" (353). She has successfully accomplished a version of the Emersonian ideal he so fervently craved when he first came to Nebraska, "happiness; to be dissolved into something complete and great" (18).

Marian overtones of universal motherhood are obvious in the scene in the orchard, where Ántonia sits within an enclosure of locust and mulberry hedges and is surrounded by adoring children and life's good things: hollyhocks and French pinks, grapevines and cherry trees, gooseberry and currant bushes, and even barnyard fowl. There is "the deepest peace in that orchard. It seemed full of sun, like a cup, and one could smell the ripe apples on the trees" (341). This della Robbia image of maternity clothed in light amid blossoms recalls Dante's dawn-bright vision of Mary in *Paradise* surrounded by festive angels and enthroned in the Mystical Rose among the saints, who from a distance resemble banks of flowers. Raising his eyes to that region of light outshining every other light, Dante beholds

... there smiling at this song and sport,
she whose beauty entered like a bliss
into the eyes of all that sainted court.

(31.133–35)

The fecundity and wisdom symbolized in the hollyhocks and mulberry support this Christian iconography while returning us to the imagery of the second book of the *Georgics*. Here Virgil celebrates the simple virtues and innocence of farm life, the yield of the fruitful earth, trees and vines, and he paints a picture of the farmer surrounded by progeny and plenty:

... happy ... is he who knows the gods
of the countryside ...
. . . .
... he sustains
His homeland, thus his little grandchildren,
His herds and trusty bullocks. ...
The seasons teem with fruits, the young of flocks,
Or sheaves of Ceres' corn; they load the furrows
And burst the barns with produce. ...
. . . .
And high on sunny terraces of rock
The mellow vintage ripens.
Meanwhile his darling children hang upon
His kisses; purity dwells in his home;
His cows have drooping udders full of milk,
And in the fresh green meadow fatling kids
Spar with their butting horns.

(2:494–528)

This is the educated townsman's idealized picture of nature lavishing her gifts on the countryman, the former's "longing for leisurely rest in broad acres or in the cool shade of Thessaly," Virgil's translator L. P. Wilkinson reminds us in his introduction to georgic 2. But Jim's idealization is motivated by longing for childhood as well as reprieve from his New York life, and he is well on his way to them within the physical harmony of this country family, whose members "were not

John and Anna Pavelka and children (no date).
Nebraska State Historical Society

afraid to touch each other" (349), whose shared memories and photographs restore to him the people and events of long ago—Jake, Otto, the Harlings, the killing of the rattler—and, as with the figures around Keats's Grecian urn, to more than they actually contain or depict. In his memory there is a "succession of . . . pictures, fixed there like the old woodcuts of one's first primer," of Ántonia in various "immemorial attitudes" (353). Among Ántonia's children, he admits feeling "like a boy, . . . and all manner of forgotten interests revived in me" (345). His final plans are to play with the Cuzak boys for a long time to come.

The central chapter (2) introduces Anton Cuzak, Ántonia's husband, speculates on their relationship, and uses it to frame the conclusion of the story of Wick Cutter and his wife. Cuzak, a city man, interested in theater and music, turned farmer to be "the instrument of Ántonia's special mission" (367), had sacrificed "the kind of life he had wanted to live" for Ántonia, who is liberal with him, lets him "drink a little too much beer in town . . . and don't say nothing, . . . don't ask . . . no questions" (365–66). Jim speculates on this practical marriage based on friendship love, the partners of which seem yokemates. This is the novel's ideal marriage, a dramatic contrast to that of the Cutters, the most grotesque of the several failed marriages Jim presents. Even here, however, aesthetic ordering is at work. The Cutters' story of hate and greed grows in horror when it is told in the Cuzak kitchen setting of love and community. It has become for the Cuzak children a shared story like the tale of the Russian wolves was for their mother and Jim. While the setting contributes to the effect of the murder and suicide, that effect contributes to the organic cohesion of this special family and further draws Jim into the family circle.

In the brief final chapter, after planning activities with his old friend's sons and resolving to pursue friendship with her husband, Jim discovers marked here and there on the rough terrain his and Ántonia's road of destiny. However inadequate or pathetic it strikes the reader as a solution to his crisis, he has become, in essence, one of her sons, yet has acquired the sons his failed marriage never gave him. Having found his family, he experiences the sense "of coming home to myself, and of having found out what a little circle man's experience is" (371–72), of connecting to nature, becoming one with "ground and sun and sky" (16). His return, his self-restoration, has its model, like so much in *My Ántonia*, in the Virgil poem Jim uses as a filter for his memoir. In the final book of the *Georgics*, Virgil fuses the story of Aristaeus' loss and recovery of his bees with the story of Orpheus' loss and abortive recovery of Eurydice. The connection between them is that Eurydice was fatally bitten by a snake while fleeing the amorous Aristaeus, thus the loss of the bees is his punishment for sexual transgression. According to the myth, bees gather their young from flowers and do not partake in destructive sex:

> . . . they forebear to indulge
> In copulation or to enervate
> Their bodies in Venus' ways. . . .
> (4:197–99)

Because "bees possess a share / Of the divine mind" (220–21), loss of bees amounts to loss of hope, the sanctity of home, the common good, virtue in general; the obvious implication is that sex relates to the serpent and to lapse and loss. (Note the association of bees with Ántonia in the fourteenth chapter of book 2 [235–37].) Such loss is a dominant theme in Cather's novel—"Whatever we had *missed*, we possessed together the precious, the incommunicable past" (372; my italics)—and Jim's coming home to himself, like the reappearance of Aristaeus' bees after proper sacrifice, becomes a restoration of hope and meaning, the discovery of a pattern, a circle (like the one in "strokes of Chinese white" [62] where the Indians used to ride), from the perspective of which the scattered pieces of life can be reassembled into a controllable order for purposes of meaning, survival, and future.

7

Conclusions and New Dimensions

Because *My Ántonia* draws significantly on Cather's life, it becomes difficult for some readers to distinguish Cather from Jim Burden, which is necessary in order to separate the concerns and themes of his story from the autobiographical subtext critics are increasingly exploring. Sifting through Jim's memoir merely to understand Cather discredits her accomplishment and reduces the novel to psychoallegory, a danger recognized by Sharon O'Brien, foremost among critics exploring the psychological subtexts of Cather's fiction, who, in *Willa Cather: The Emerging Voice,* cautions against presuming that the overt texts always conceal covert texts, which are the "real" stories. *My Ántonia* actually contains three rather than two stories: the one Jim constructs, the story generating this construction, and Cather's own story.

Cather emphatically distances herself from Jim in the introduction, where she presents him as a separate person with a "romantic disposition which often made him seem very funny as a boy." Jim's inability to see all that Cather sees is underscored in the second book when Frances Harling tells him she knows the country girls better than he does: "You always put a kind of glamour over them. The trouble with you, Jim, is that you're romantic" (229). This echoes part of

Cather's estimate in the introduction; the rest is echoed by Lena Lingard when she surrenders Jim to Gaston Cleric and Harvard: "I used to think I'd like to be your first sweetheart. You were such a funny kid!" (293). Also, Cather allows Jim to contradict himself in condemning Black Hawk's "respect for respectability" (202) before confessing, "Disapprobation hurt me, I found—even that of people whom I did not admire" (228). Once we make the distinction between Jim and his creator we must grapple with what he tells us about himself as well as what she is telling us about him. Jim's immediate task in mid-life is to make his past special, meaningful enough to fill an otherwise empty present life, a task involving perception, arrangement, and interpretation.

Heightening the events of that past is one way to fill the present void, and Jim learns how to achieve this while a student in Lincoln by using literature as a filter for viewing life. To the extent that he succeeds, however, he separates himself from the real world and occupies one of his own making, a process ironically contributing to the condition it is later used to alleviate. Examining the changes in Jim's perception of reality as the result of the aesthetic conditioning described in the third book is crucial to understanding the novel. The first two books benefit positively from an artistic sensibility: Jim handles language well, uses detail to advantage, and employs pictorial techniques. In the last two books, however, reality becomes decidedly secondary to poetry. The funeral of Mr. Shimerda is a moving piece of realistic art, as is the picnic with the hired girls (even during the climactic moment when the plow is magnified by the sun), but the farewell between Jim and Ántonia with the moon and sun in the sky is self-consciously theatrical, as if the sentimentality generated through rhythmic language, romantic imagery, and rendering of landscape in "that singular light" (322) is intended to hide the cruelty of Jim's departure and somehow fill the gaping emptiness he was creating for himself at the time. Surely this scene is not an example of Cather's memory-clothed realism. It is the mawkish product of quiet despair (and perhaps a parody of her own early attitudes and writing). To a lesser extent, the same estimate can be made of the poetic flights in the first chapter of the last book.

Arrangement and selection also enhance the meaning of Jim's story, which traces a descending curve of shorter and shorter books. The first two books record the fullness of his childhood and adolescence with Ántonia and other friends; the third, the turning from life to letters and departure from Lena; the last two, how he compensates for the emptiness of the course chosen in book 3. The first two comprise two-thirds of the novel, which is appropriate for what is essentially a memoir of childhood; consequently, the final third should indicate why childhood is the happiest part of Jim's life.

Book 1 divides into four parts. The first (chaps. 1–3) is an introduction to the setting and characters; the second (chaps. 4–8) anticipates winter through killing frosts and the chilling story of the wolves; the third (chaps. 9–16), the winter section, frames Christmas celebrations and the tragic climax, the suicide of Mr. Shimerda; the fourth (chaps. 17–19) propels the reader from the bleak funeral and into spring. Book 2 also divides into four parts. The first (chaps. 1–5), as in the first book, introduces setting and characters; the second (chaps. 6–7), a winter section, frames the tramp's suicide and the Blind d'Arnault concert; the third (chaps. 8–12), the climactic section, dramatizes the struggle between puberty and small-town restraint that erupts when Ántonia quits the Harlings'; the fourth (chaps. 13–15) contains Jim's picnic with the hired girls before concluding with the "rape" scene, the outcome of Ántonia's going to the Cutters'. Book 3 is the novel's turning point: after establishing the influence on him of Gaston Cleric and the classics, Jim develops his relationship with Lena but then follows Cleric to Harvard. Book 4 repeats the pattern of book 3: Jim hears the story of Ántonia's disgrace before declaring his affection for her and again departing for Harvard. Book 5 contains the image of children exploding from the cave, the revitalization of life sought by Jim in his attempt to resume his relationship with Ántonia, make her into an archetype, and reconnect to nature and his lost past.

Many parallels and connections become evident in the memoir Jim designs for us: the winter sections in books 1 and 2 are balanced in the celebratory and tragic events they frame; Jim's struggle with the snake in book 1 recurs in his struggle with Cutter in book 2; the burial of Mr. Shimerda in book 1 anticipates the explosion from the cave in book 5; Mrs. Steavens's narrative of Ántonia's disgrace in book 4 echoes Grandfather Burden's reading of the Christmas story in book 1; Lena's renunciation of Jim in book 3 prefigures his farewell scene with Antonia in book 4. Making these and additional connections indicates the sophisticated form of an apparently casual narrative and begins to expose the exclusiveness and sexual reticence that make Jim's mid-life so empty.

Jim's romantic disposition is perhaps most obvious in his interpretation of the events of his life. Emerson says in "History" that "the whole of history is in one man," that "it is all to be explained from individual experience." The miniature experiences of each man parallel the primitive ages, Greek history, the era of chivalry, the days of maritime adventure and circumnavigation, and so forth. "Civil history, natural history, the history of art and the history of literature," he continues, "all must be explained from individual history, or must remain words." Jim's life encapsulates a significant period of America's story, an exciting one of country-building that he traces in his movement from prairie to town and town to city, from a close-to-nature life with Ántonia to frequenting the theater in Lincoln with Lena. But the American historical pattern is merely its surface; beneath it lies a version of the myth of man's emergence, fall, and triumph.

After rejecting his popular "Jesse James" story as an inadequate measure of his new experience, Jim surrenders himself completely to nature, to the empty, rolling terrain and gigantic sky, to the state of things before countries were made, as if somehow he were witnessing the world emerging from chaos. He then introduces vegetation and animals and travels to the Shimerda dugout to watch humanity arise from the earth itself. One member of the Shimerda family, Marek, provides a link between human and animal life, and Ántonia herself is closely connected to the earth from which she originates. The civilizing function of language, the primary tool of his art, is evident when Jim names himself and items in the landscape for the Shimerda girls. Increasingly cold weather soon transforms the glorious autumnal land into a foreboding and increasingly alien place for Mr. Shimerda, a figure of dejection in the sunset. Jim then struggles with the serpent in the prairie-dog town, a situation occasioned by Ántonia and reminding us that Eve involved Adam with Satan. The ancient "Evil" Jim associates with the rattler becomes evident in the sinful nature of Peter and Pavel's tossing the bride and groom to the wolves. While the winter landscape, quarreling between the Shimerdas and Burdens, Mr. Shimerda's death, and disputes about his burial are symptoms of a fallen world, hope is introduced through the lighted Christmas tree and the creche figures hung on it, the stiff paper Christ child juxtaposing the rigid corpse of the suicide. The subsequent spring brings seasonal resurrection, and the Shimerdas continue their evolution by moving into a house above ground. Ántonia's intimacy with the earth develops as she works the soil and is browned by the sun.

The Burdens' move to town, although socially an improvement, is actually a lapse, a distancing from innocent nature. Jim learns to fight and tease girls, and Ántonia is exposed to the variety of influences that eventually bring about her ruin. The serpent here is personified in the lecherous money lender, Wick Cutter. Lena's entrance as a Venus figure announces that puberty rather than cold has become the challenge. Fallen humanity is evident when defoliation uncovers the social prejudices and cruelties of the town. Winter frames Ántonia's tale of the misfit tramp who committed suicide and of grotesque pianist Blind d'Arnault's transferrence of sexual energy to the piano. Soon the innocents are expelled from the Harling garden. Ántonia, too trusting and loving for a fallen world, is the first to go. Her sexuality leads to employment by Satan himself, Wick Cutter, and involvement with the womanizing railroad conductor who eventually ruins her. The picnic with the hired girls is a brief respite, a recapitulation of human aspirations, some already thwarted, before the town section ends on a note of chaos and anger after Cutter's attack on Jim.

Growing sophistication, modern man's separation from vital life forces, is represented in Jim falling under the influence of Cleric and learning to use literature as a substitute for life. Although strongly tempted by Venus in the person of Lena to come out of his solitude and aestheticism, Jim is able to transfer his passions to a play and remain personally inviolable. Confirmed in his ability to protect himself from close relationships, Jim returns to the fallen Ántonia after hearing her story given biblical dimensions by Mrs. Steavens. Making Ántonia into a saintly if disgraced mother, Jim fixes her in his mind as an icon to carry with him all the days of his life. His confession that the "idea" rather than the reality of her is "part of [his] mind" (321) recalls the romantic ravings of the narrator of Poe's "Ligeia" about his first wife. Like the narrator, Jim is able, twenty years later, to make the real woman, now battered, conform to his idealization. In a grand creative gesture he overcomes physical reality, reworks the icon into a kind of Coronation of the Virgin with Ántonia at the center of her orchard, and washes it all of sex—the serpent has been crushed. What was lost he imagines found; what has lapsed he feels restored. Ántonia's children explode from the fruit cave and dizzy him. Resurrection is accomplished. Mr. Shimerda lives again in the fawnlike grandson who plays his violin.

As a true romantic Jim imagines and constructs his history with Ántonia into a miniature of man's, fills his emptiness, and enables himself to carry on. Such is the essence of the novel's optimism. What is pessimistic is the need for the effort, that so much was missed in Jim's life and in his relationships with Ántonia and Lena.

A clue to what Cather is telling us about Jim is evident, I think, in his final sentence: "Whatever we had missed, we possessed together the precious, the incommunicable past." I would emphasize the first four words, because the key to Jim's story is in what he had missed and how he reconciles himself to it by filling the emptiness with something else. Cather's comment about the pattern of *My Ántonia* to Flora Merrill in a 1925 interview is an illuminating addendum to its final sentence. This novel, she said, "is just the other side of the rug, the pattern that is supposed not to count in a story. In it there is no love affair, no courtship, nor marriage, no broken heart, no struggle for success. I knew I'd ruin my material if I put it in the usual fictional pattern. I just used it the way I thought absolutely true." What is the material? How does it relate to all that is missing? These are the questions readers must ask. They are central to Cather's method in this and other novels. A paragraph from one of her rare statements on writing, "The Novel Demeuble," provides at least the semblance of an answer:

> Whatever is felt upon the page without being specifically named there—that, one might say, is created. It is the inexplicable presence of the thing not named, of the overtone divined by the ear but not heard by it, the verbal mood, the emotional aura of the fact or the thing or the deed, that gives high quality to the novel or the drama, as well as to poetry itself.

What is communicated to the careful reader of Jim's story is an empty life like the one Tennyson's persona finds lamentable at the end of *In Memoriam* 27:

> I hold it true, whate'er befall;
> I feel it, when I sorrow most;
> 'Tis better to have loved and lost
> Than never to have loved at all.

Jim's story also can be illuminated by another Victorian chestnut, Whittier's "Maud Muller," which tells the story of a wealthy lawyer who fell in love with a country girl of "feet so bare, and . . . tattered gown" but married "a wife of richest dower, / Who lived for fashion, as he for power." Many years later, "when many children played round [the] door" of work-worn Maud, who had married a poor farmer, the wealthy judge watched in his fireplace:

> . . . a picture come and go;
>
> And Sweet Maud Muller's hazel eyes
> Looked out in their innocent surprise.
> . . . .
> And closed his eyes on his garnished rooms
> To dream of meadows and clover-blooms.
> . . . .
> God pity them both; and pity us all,
> Who vainly the dreams of youth recall.

> For of all sad words of tongue or pen,
> The saddest are these: "It might have been!"

Ántonia, unlike Maud, is not a candidate for pity, but the successful yet unfulfilled judge and Jim are. Whether or not we lament Jim's abandonment of Lena in Lincoln or of Ántonia at her father's grave, we must conclude, in light of the information the introduction provides, that Jim's life is unhappy and that this has motivated his quest for childhood.

Although I began this conclusion encouraging readers to abide by the separation Cather emphatically makes between Jim Burden and herself in the introduction, it must be acknowledged that some readers cannot or refuse to do so. Some cannot accept a female novelist's construction of a convincing male perspective and cite as evidence incidents like Jim's failure to generate sexual passion for Ántonia; his emotional response to the lovers during the performance of *Camille:* "I wept unrestrainedly . . . ; the handkerchief in my breast-pocket, worn for elegance . . . , was wet through . . ." (277); his insistence before the snake killing that "I was a boy and [Ántonia] was a girl" (43), and his overreaction to Wick Cutter's attack: "I hated her. . . . She had let me in for all this disgustingness" (250). Such macho predilection, which challenges as well the viability of characters like Lawrence Selden in Edith Wharton's *The House of Mirth,* John Fincastle in Ellen Glasgow's *Vein of Iron,* and other female creations of males is, ironically, perilously close to some feminist attempts to collapse the distinction between Cather and Jim in order to read the novel as an exploration of Cather's erotic desire for other women. This is the approach taken by Deborah Lambert (see my chap. 3), in which Jim becomes a mask for Cather's erotic attachment to Annie Pavelka, a presumption unsupported by biographical fact. Despite the hints of sexual "deviancy" in her deep attachments to Louise Pound and Isabelle McClung, I have hesitated to refer to Cather as a lesbian writer because such a conclusion remains speculative among cautious scholars, and because revealing such speculations at the outset can reduce *My Ántonia* and other Cather novels to narcissistic psychoallegories.

A careful and representative treatment of this issue is the O'Brien study mentioned earlier, although it offers only scattered if perceptive comments on *My Ántonia*.

Cather's recurrent theme according to this thesis is the mother–daughter bond, that her difficulty in relating to her mother, Virginia, was complicated by the latter's domineering traits and Southern belle proprieties, the family exodus from Virginia to Nebraska, and Cather's lesbian identity. Using psychological studies by Nancy Chodorow and other feminist writers, O'Brien explains that daughters face greater difficulties than sons in establishing autonomy from their mothers because there is no gender barrier between them, and how in Cather's case this threat led to early rebellion against the ladylike role expected of her, and then, after the migration to Nebraska, the assuming of a male persona. The uprooting from Virginia signified separation from the mother and subsequent abandonment in the prairie wasteland, where Virginia Cather was reduced to helplessness due to pregnancy complications and inability to domesticate the space around her. Cather's reaction to the sense of helplessness she at first shared with her mother caused her to identify with men, whom she associated with power and creativity, and to substitute her mother with immigrant farm women adept at making gardens in the wilderness, whose kitchens duplicated the domestic space she remembered in Virginia.

Cather's pleasant memories of her Nebraska childhood were the result of the relative freedom of postpioneer society and the fact that young children are neither very male nor very female, which enabled her to play the boy's role and accomplish the ambitions she shaped from the romantic heroes of her reading. Aspiring to be a doctor she christened herself William Cather, M.D., taking as role models Red Cloud's two physicians, McKeeby and Damerell. Yet this transformation, while distinguishing her from her Victorian lady mother, can be interpreted as an expression of desire for her mother's love. "As William she could rival the males her mother favored, competing with her father, her brothers and the new baby," writes O'Brien. "Moreover, as William she could join the competition for maternal affection without fearing the 'erasure of personality' she found terrifying, protecting herself from merging and sameness by the same action that declared her

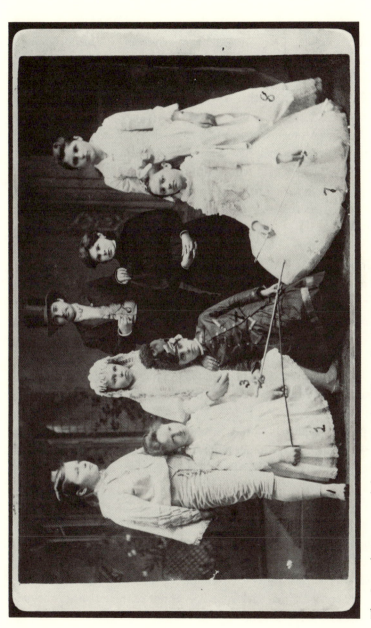

The Cast of "Beauty and the Beast" with Willa as the Merchant Father.
Nebraska State Historical Society

attachment. As her mother's son, the daughter could both receive and seek her mother's love without being crippled by dependency and powerlessness." This fear of erasure was particularly terrifying to Cather because of her lesbian identity.

O'Brien uses the Cather–Lousie Pound correspondence (at Duke University Library) to establish Cather's awareness of the deviance associated with women whose erotic-emotional ties are primarily with other women. Late nineteenth-century recognition that women are capable of passion brought with it suspicion about attachments considered innocent in earlier times. Cather's complaint in a letter to Pound that such love is considered unnatural indicates her recognition of the stigma attached to it, awareness perhaps aggravated by the male persona she had assumed. Her lesbian identification further complicated her relationship with her mother because it involved the erotic bond that a heterosexual daughter would have transferred to her father and other males. Therefore, Cather's desire for union with her mother threatened her autonomy with total fusion and engulfment. The forbidden passionate relationship was then compensated for in relationships with other women, who became mother substitutes. Isabelle McClung, the romance of her life, was Cather's primary mother substitute but without her own mother's authority to dominate and threaten her.

Cather employed various strategies in her fiction to satisfy her need to return to her mother without endangering her autonomy and without revealing "deviant" eroticism. Foremost among these was the use of male characters as masks to explore love for her mother and other women. In an early story "The Burglar's Christmas," for example, a prodigal son named William returns home to his fashionable mother who threatens his existence with passionate embraces described in the language of romantic fiction. While O'Brien insists that this relationship is a simple cover for the mother–daughter relationship, she concedes that such simplicity is not characteristic of the mature fiction and suggests the

> need to develop interpretive strategies for determining when a male character is a "mask" rather than an opposite-sex character whom

> Cather created by drawing, in part, on herself. . . . I suggest that only if textual clues contradict or question the male character's assigned gender can we proclaim him a "mask" or "cover." . . . By contrast, a character like Godfrey St. Peter in *The Professor's House*, however "feminine" his sensibility, should be considered male. . . . In stories where textual clues direct us to consider the male characters as masks for a female perceiver, the heterosexual "cover" story functions simultaneously as disguise and defense and serves a social as well as a psychological function. . . . Cather's early stories call for the same interpretive strategy required by most of her fiction. Since at times she was writing two stories at once, a heterosexual and a homosexual one, . . . we are frequently faced with indeterminate meaning rather than with a clearly encoded subtext that constitutes the "real" message of the text. The heterosexual "cover" story, although socially necessary as a way of naming indirectly the "thing not named" [lesbian love], is not invariably the false one, the hidden lesbian story the real. Instead, meaning and authorial intention oscillate back and forth between the two.

Cather persisted in using the male perspective throughout her career, despite the complaint of her mentor Sarah Orne Jewett that "when a woman writes in the man's character,—it must always . . . be something of a masquerade." O'Brien insists that Cather's penchant for male narrators and personas does not presume her male identification, that such identification was not the consequence of her lesbianism; however, if we conclude that Cather is lesbian we must acknowledge her lesbianism as contributing to her use of male personas to conceal it.

O'Brien detects attraction to both the nurturing and erotic aspects of women in Cather's 1895 review of paintings from the Chicago Art Institute, in which she singles out portraits of women by an obscure Pennsylvania painter Carl Newman and Frank Benson's painting of a girl in the firelight as "ecstatically beautiful" and "best seen in solitude. . . . It is a privilege and a blessing to be alone with such divine femininities. . . ." She notes Benson's girl as defined by the shoulders and Newman's women by the bust, that one of the latter figures is of cruder stock than Benson's, has warmer sympathies, more strength but less energy: "She has a liberal share of muscle and adipose tissue, while the other is all nerves. Benson's girl is all lightness and poise." Cather then rhapsodizes on the Benson: "What a girl she is anyway! What simplicity and elegance. How the slenderness of the waist, the poise of the head, the carriage, the firmness of the flesh, even the severe elegance of the dress with its little cloud of wonderfully painted illusion about the breast combine to suggest that innate aristocratic refinement which should be the outcome of wealth and culture." O'Brien perceptively links the Newman figure with Ántonia and the immigrant women who mothered Cather in Nebraska, and in the Benson she sees the elegance of Cather's own mother, Louise Pound, and Isabelle McClung. While nurturing and erotic elements are fused in this interpretation, one of Cather's strategies is to divide her heroines into maternal and erotic figures, as in *O Pioneers!*, between Alexandra and Marie, and in *My Ántonia*, between Ántonia and Lena. This division, like the male mask, offers protection for the lesbian writer from the incestuous consequences of erotic relationship with the maternal figure.

In applying the above aspects of O'Brien's thesis to *My Ántonia*, we must consider Jim as a mask for Cather, or at best a twin brother alter ego, despite her insistence in the introduction on his separate identity. Jim's search for a mothering figure then becomes Cather's, and his being orphaned reflects her feelings of abandonment after she arrived in Nebraska. Grandmother Burden, who tends a garden and whose kitchen is a domestic oasis in a desert, assumes the role of the immigrant pioneer women who mothered Cather during her first Nebraska year. Also, Jim's desire to dissolve into nature represents Cather's ambivalent desire for fusion with her mother, his glorification of childhood innocence reflects hers, and his contrasting relationships with Ántonia and Lena indicate strategies to cover or avoid what is erotic in the mother–daughter relationship.

The beginning of the novel's first book dramatizes both the desire for the mother and the determination to preserve autonomy. Equating such desire with religious ecstasy, sexual union, and death (as does O'Brien) relates it to Jim's "happiness" in his grandmother's sunny garden: "Perhaps we feel like that when we die and become a part of something entire . . . , dissolved into something complete and great" (18). This "something" desired seems to be symbolized in mother earth itself, although the sheltered draw-bottom in which Jim lounges qualifies that desire in protecting the boundaries of his selfhood from complete dissolution. Dual tendencies for natural shelters and fusion punctuate the entire novel: Jim is "reluctant to leave [the] green enclosure where the sunlight flickered so bright" (234) to join the hired girls for the picnic; during his farewell scene with Ántonia, he "felt the old pull of the earth [and] . . . wished [he] could be a little boy again, and that [his] way could end there" (322); the suicide's grave at the crossroads is "the spot most dear" to him "in all that country" (119), and near the end, Ántonia's orchard, "full of sun like a cup" (341), parallels Grandmother Burden's sheltered garden. Mother and earth fuse in the earth tones which paint Ántonia "a stalwart, brown woman" (331); in her proximity to the earth ("I like to be . . . where all the ground is friendly" [320]); and in the "veritable explosion of life out of the dark [nurturing] cave [of her womb] into the sunlight" (339). Enshrining Ántonia as mother earth within the orchard enables Cather (through Jim) to fuse with the mother (he wants "to play [with Ántonia's boys] for a long while" [370]) while preserving the autonomy of selfhood.

As part of Cather's strategy to sanitize and defuse union with the mother for Jim and herself, for both cases would involve erotic love and, especially for the lesbian daughter, loss of selfhood, the mother–child relationship is washed of passion. O'Brien's speculation that in Cather the lesbian daughter's and the oedipal son's desire for the mother is punishable by castration provides a clue to the mutilating potential of Lena Lingard. The danger posed by Lena's reaping hook in Jim's dream of her can be interpreted as a warning to him to restrict sexual activity to her, since this would not involve the same guilt as would sex with Ántonia. This explains why she disrupts Jim and Ántonia's tête-à-tête during the picnic and tells Jim in Lincoln, "I used to think I'd like to be your first sweetheart" (293). The threat of mutilation seems unrelated to making love to her: "Lena Lingard came across the stubble barefoot, in a short skirt, with a curved reaping-hook in her hand. . . . She sat down beside me, turned to me with a soft sigh and said, 'Now they are all gone, and I can kiss you as much as I like'" (225–26). Restricting sexual response to Lena separates it from the childbearing and nurturing activities associated with Ántonia, which is why, despite himself, Jim cannot have "this flattering dream about Ántonia" (226). Sexual response to Ántonia is out of the question by the time Jim recalls his dream of Lena and omits the now unnecessary reaping hook: "my old dream about Lena coming across the harvest-field in her short skirt seemed to me like the memory of an actual experience" (271).

Jim labels his reminiscence of Lena with the mournful line from Virgil's *Georgics*, "*Optima dies . . . prima fugit,*" to revive the androgynous days of childhood, when he played without guilt in the Harlings' sun-filled garden. These were the days before girls were very female or boys were very male, when Cather herself could be her own twin brother and Jim one of the girls. But that happiest spring, when "the apple and cherry trees broke into bloom [and the children] ran about under them, hunting for the new nests the birds were building, throwing clods at each other, and playing hide and seek," was ending: "The summer which was to change everything was coming nearer every day. When boys and girls are growing up, life can't stand still, not even in the quietest of country towns; and they have to grow up, whether they will or no" (193).

My Ántonia, then, can be approached from inward or outward perspectives, can be directed toward Cather's life or beyond it and even beyond the emptiness of Jim's life. The contour of either direction is the circular road bringing Jim, Cather, and the reader home. I prefer to give that journey the scope of Ulysses' in canto 26 of Dante's *Hell*, whose passage through the womblike Straits of Gibraltar and toward death in unknown seas begins and ends in maternal engulfment. Nautical imagery abounds in Ulysses' account, from winglike oars propelling the ship westward and the tempest following the appearance of Purgatory across the watery expanse, to the sea closing over the crew's heads, and the bow whirling into churning waters. Jim's voyage, also westward, is through a sea of Nebraska grass: "As I looked about me

112

I felt that the grass was the country, as the water is the sea. The red of the grass made all the great prairie the colour of wine-stains, or of certain seaweeds when they are first washed up" (15). As he travels to his grandparents' farm on that first night, there is "nothing but land . . . slightly undulating" (7). Like Ulysses, he feels beyond the confines of civilized life: "I had the feeling that the world was left behind, that we had got over the edge of it, and were outside man's jurisdiction." There is in both men a curious blend of ego-building and self-effacement. The punished Ulysses comments on how it "pleased [God's] will" to answer his ambition with obliterating seas. Jim feels "erased, blotted out" (8), but also expresses a desire for annihilation: "I wanted to walk straight on through the red grass and over the edge of the world, which could not be very far away. The light air about me told me that the world ended here: only the grass and sun and sky were left, and if one went a little farther there would be only sun and sky, and one would float off into them, like the tawny hawks which sailed over our heads making slow shadows on the grass" (16). Both experiences betray conflict between the comfort of circumscribed vision or space—the sheltered Mediterranean world and the prairie garden—and the dissolving outward Emily Dickinson refers to as circumference.

Or perhaps Cather's model is the journey of Walt Whitman, whose poetry so influenced her fiction. In "Song of Myself" he imaged spiritual birth as passage through the flexible doors of life's womb and final destiny as union with the "great Camerado." In "Passage to India" he envisioned human destiny as fusion with God: "love complete, the Elder Brother found, / The Younger melts in fondness in her arms." The road home here, as in Cather, successfully juxtaposes fusion and selfhood. Doubtlessly all such journeys arise from psychic pressures and maladjustments, but somehow they explode beyond sex, beyond time, beyond the claustrophobic lives of authors.

Appendix A: Pavelka Letter

[This letter was written by Annie Pavelka (the prototype of Ántonia), two months before her death at the age of eighty-six, to Frances Samland, Omaha, Nebraska, a student of Gunnar Horn, Benson High School.]

Bladen [Nebraska] February 24–1955

Dear Frantiska

recieved your nice and wellcome letter few days ago, thought I would please you and answer your queastions about our coming to this country from Bohemia 75 years ago last November the 5. we started from our vilage Mzizovice [?] 16th of October 1880 and got to Red Cloud in November 5 we were on the water 11 days, there was another Bohemia family came with us, rest on the ship were pollish, my father wanted to bring us to this country so we would have it better here as he used to hear how good it was hear as he had letters from here how wonderfull it was out here that there were beautiful houses lot of trees and so on, but how disapointed he was when he saw them pretty houses duged in the banks of the deep draws. You couldnt see them untill you came rite to the door just steel chimmeny in the roof. there were no roads Just tracks from wagon wheels peaple cut acros land to get anywhere at all well we came to Joe Polnickys by hiring a man at Red Cloud, and from there Mr. Polnicky took us out to Charlie Krecek that's the one who wrote so nice about Nebraska and behold our surprise in sieng such beuttiful building and our first meal there was corn meal mush and molasses that was what the peaple lived on and wild

115

fowls and rabbits well my father boght 10060 acker farm, there was nothing on it exept sod shack it had Just a board bed and 4 lid stove, no well Just 5 aikers of land broken that much the first homsteder had to ow [?] when he didn't live there all time Just so many months so he could realy own it but the folks didnt live there they moved in with some Jerman family. and that was a bad winter lots of snow not much to cook nothing to burn no place to go nothing to read peaple had to burn corn stalk sunflowers and cow chips it was lucky mother brought feather beds as we had to sleep on the dirt floors with hay for mattres, that was hard on father in the old country he had weaver when it was cold and in the evenings he would sit and make linens and any kind of wearing material allways and was allways Joking and happy he was a man in a milion allways had lots of friend I was allways with when there was anything to do allways called me naminka, and mother maminka he never swore or used dirty words like other men nor he never drank or play cards he was a clean man in everyway. then one nice afternoon it was 15 of feb he told mother he was going to hunt rabbits he brought a shot gun from the old country he never used it here nobody dared to shoot when he didnt return by fiveo clock mother older brother and the man we lived with went to look for him it was dark when they found him half siting in the old house back of the bed shot in the head and allready cold nearly frozen the sherif said it was a suiside there no cemetery or nothing one of the near neghbors had to make a wooden box and they had to make his grave in the corner of our farm but my brother him moved and him and my mother and brother are sleeping in Red Cloud cemetery and they have a tumbstone I hope they are restting sweetly. most all is true that you read in the Book thoug most of the names are changed, our name was Sadilek, Lena Lidgard was Mary Dusek my friend Kid Clutter was Willa's cousin. and was a good looking cowboy gues I will close for this time I hope this will help you in anyway.

Your friend   Mrs. Pavelka

Appendix B: "Peter"

[This short story, "Peter," was written when Cather was a college freshman and published in the *Mahogany Tree* in May 1892. It is based on the suicide of Frank Sadilek, the father of Annie, the prototype of Ántonia.]

"No, Antone, I have told thee many, many times, no, thou shalt not sell it until I am gone."

"But I need money; what good is that old fiddle to thee? The very crows laugh at thee when thou art trying to play. Thy hand trembles so thou canst scarce hold the bow. Thou shalt go with me to the Blue to cut wood tomorrow. See to it thou art up early."

"What, on the Sabbath, Antone, when it is so cold? I get so very cold, my son, let us not go tomorrow."

"Yes, tomorrow, thou lazy old man. Do not cut wood upon the Sabbath? Care I how cold it is? Wood thou shalt cut, and haul it too, and as for the fiddle, I tell thee I will sell it yet." Antone pulled his ragged cap down over his low, heavy brow, and went out. The old man drew his stool up nearer the fire, and sat stroking his violin with trembling fingers and muttering, "Not while I live, not while I live."

Five years ago they had come here, Peter Sadelack, and his wife, and oldest son Antone, and countless smaller Sadelacks, here to south-western Nebraska, and had taken up a homestead. Antone was the acknowledged master of the premises, and people said he was a likely youth, and would do well. That he was mean and untrustworthy every one knew, but that made little difference. His corn was better tended than any in the country, and his wheat always yielded more than other men's.

117

Of Peter no one knew much, nor had any one a good word to say for him. He drank whenever he could get out of Antone's sight long enough to pawn his hat or coat for whiskey. Indeed there were but two things he would not pawn, his pipe and violin. He was a lazy, absent-minded old fellow, who liked to fiddle better than to plow, though Antone surely got work enough out of them all, for that matter. In the house of which Antone was master there was no one, from the little boy three years old, to the old man of sixty, who did not earn his bread. Still people said that Peter was worthless, and was a great drag on Antone, his son, who never drank, and was a much better man than his father had ever been. Peter did not care what people said. He did not like the country, nor the people, least of all he liked the plowing. He was very homesick for Bohemia. Long ago, only eight years ago by the calendar, but it seemed eight centuries to Peter, he had been a second violinist in the great theatre at Prague. He had gone into the theatre very young, and had been there all his life, until he had a stroke of paralysis, which made his arms so weak that his bowing was uncertain. Then they told him he could go. Those were great days at the theatre. He had plenty to drink then, and wore a dress coat every evening, and there were always parties after the play. He could play in those days, ay, that he could! He could never read the notes well, so he did not play first; but his touch, he had a touch indeed, so Herr Mikilsdoff, who led the orchestra, had said. Sometimes now Peter thought he could plow better if he could only bow as he used to. He had seen all the lovely women in the world there, all the great singers and the great players. He was in the orchestra when Rachel played, and he heard Liszt play when the Countess d'Agoult sat in the stage box and threw the master white lilies. Once, a French woman came and played for weeks, he did not remember her name now. He did not remember her face very well either, for it changed so, it was never twice the same. But the beauty of it, and the great hunger men felt at the sight of it, that he remembered. Most of all he remembered her voice. He did not know French, and could not understand a word she said, but it seemed to him that she must be talking the music of Chopin. And her voice, he thought he should know that in the other world. The last night she played a play in which a man touched her arm and she stabbed him. As Peter sat among the smoking gas jets down below the footlights with his fiddle on his knee, and looked up to her, he thought he would like to die, too, if he could touch her arm once, and have her stab him so. Peter went home to his wife very drunk that night. Even in those days he was a foolish fellow, who cared for nothing but music and pretty faces.

It was all different now. He had nothing to drink and little to eat, and here, there was nothing but sun, and grass, and sky. He had forgotten almost everything, but some things he remembered well enough. He loved his violin and the holy Mary, and above all else he feared the Evil One, and his son Antone.

The fire was low, and it grew cold. Still Peter sat by the fire remembering. He dared not throw more cobs on the fire; Antone would be angry. He did not want to cut wood tomorrow, it would be Sunday, and he wanted to go to mass. Antone might let him do that. He held his violin under his wrinkled chin, his white hair fell over it, and he began to play "Ave Maria." His hand shook more than ever before, and at last refused to work the bow at all. He sat stupefied for awhile, then rose, and taking his violin with him, stole out into the old stable. He took Antone's shot-gun down from its peg, and loaded it by the moonlight which streamed in through the door. He sat down on the dirt floor, and leaned back against the dirt wall. He heard the wolves howling in the distance, and the night wind screaming as it swept over the snow. Near him he heard the regular breathing of the horses in the dark. He put his crucifix above his heart, and folding his hands said brokenly all the Latin he had ever known, "Pater noster, qui in coelum est." Then he raised his head and sighed, "Not one kreutzer will Antone pay them to pray for my soul, not one kreutzer, he is so careful of his money, is Antone; he does not waste it in drink, he is a better man than I, but hard sometimes; he works the girls too hard; women were not made to work so; but he shall not sell thee, my fiddle, I can play thee not more, but they shall not part us; we have seen it all together, and we will forget it together, the French woman and all." He held his fiddle under his chin a moment, where it had lain so often, then put it across his knee and broke it through the middle. He pulled off his old boot, held the gun between his knees with the muzzle against his forehead, and pressed the trigger with his toe.

In the morning Antone found him stiff, frozen fast in a pool of blood. They could not straighten him out enough to fit a coffin, so they buried him in a pine box. Before the funeral Antone carried to town the fiddlebow which Peter had forgotten to break. Antone was very thrifty, and a better man than his father had been.

Selected Bibliography

Primary Works

Fiction

Collected Short Fiction, 1892–1912. Rev. ed. Edited by Virginia Faulkner. Lincoln: University of Nebraska Press, 1970. Includes *The Troll Garden* (1905) stories.

Alexander's Bridge. Boston: Houghton Mifflin, 1912; Lincoln: University of Nebraska Press, 1977.

O Pioneers! Boston: Houghton Mifflin, 1913; Sentry Edition, 1962.

The Song of the Lark. Boston: Houghton Mifflin, 1915; Sentry (revised, 1932) Edition, 1963.

Uncle Valentine and Other Stories: Willa Cather's Uncollected Short Fiction, 1915–1929. Edited by Benice Slote. Lincoln: University of Nebraska Press, 1973.

My Ántonia. Boston: Houghton Mifflin, 1918; Sentry Edition, 1961.

Youth and the Bright Medusa. New York: Knopf, 1920; New York: Vintage, 1976. Seven stories of artistic temperaments.

One of Ours. New York: Knopf, 1922; New York: Vintage, 1971.

A Lost Lady. New York: Knopf, 1923; New York: Vintage, 1972.

The Professor's House. New York: Knopf, 1925; New York: Vintage, 1973.

My Mortal Enemy. New York: Knopf, 1926; New York: Vintage, 1961.

Death Comes for the Archbishop. New York: Knopf, 1927; New York: Vintage, 1971.

Shadows on the Rock. New York: Knopf, 1931; New York: Vintage, 1971.

Obscure Destinies. New York: Knopf, 1932; New York: Vintage, 1974. Three long short stories.

Lucy Gayheart. New York: Knopf, 1935; New York: Vintage, 1976.

Sapphira and the Slave Girl. New York: Knopf, 1940; New York: Vintage, 1975.

The Old Beauty and Others. New York: Knopf, 1948; New York: Vintage, 1976. The last three stories.

Poetry

April Twilights (1903). Rev. ed. Edited by Bernice Slote. Lincoln: University of Nebraska Press, 1968.

Nonfiction

The Kingdom of Art: Willa Cather's First Principles and Critical Statements, 1893–1896. Edited by Bernice Slote. Lincoln: University of Nebraska Press, 1966. Cather's dramatic and literary criticism.

The World and the Parish: Willa Cather's Articles and Reviews, 1893–1902. Edited by William M. Curtin. Lincoln: University of Nebraska Press, 1970.

Not Under Forty. New York: Knopf, 1936. Essays on writing and literature.

Willa Cather in Europe. New York: Knopf, 1956. Fourteen travel articles.

Willa Cather on Writing. New York: Knopf, 1949. Essays on writing and literature.

Willa Cather in Person: Interviews, Speeches, and Letters. Edited by L. Brent Bohlke. Lincoln: University of Nebraska Press, 1986. Traces Cather's public responses to her career and the writing and state of fiction.

Secondary Works

Biographical Studies

Bennett, Mildred R. *The World of Willa Cather*. New York: Dodd, Mead, 1951; Lincoln: University of Nebraska Press, 1961. Of primary value in understanding the influence of childhood associations in the fiction.

Brown, E. K., and Leon Edel. *Willa Cather: A Critical Biography*. New York: Knopf, 1953. Combines the biography with critical introduction to major works, clarifying the autobiographical nature of much of the fiction and concern for fiction as a fine art.

Byrne, Kathleen D., and Richard C. Snyder. *Chrysalis: Willa Cather in Pittsburgh*. Pittsburgh: Historical Society of Western Pennsylvania, 1980. Focuses on author's ten years in Pittsburgh as teacher and journalist and her relationship to the McClung family.

Lewis, Edith. *Willa Cather Living*. New York: Knopf, 1953. Companion volume to Brown/Edel, generous with glimpses into the author's life provided by the woman who shared that life.

Sergeant, Elizabeth Shepley. *Willa Cather: A Memoir*. Philadelphia: J. B. Lippincott, 1953; Lincoln: University of Nebraska Press, 1963. Valuable, but as one writer's remembrances of another the focus is often blurred.

Woodress, James. *Willa Cather: A Literary Life*. Lincoln: University of Nebraska Press, 1987. Updates, combines, and supplements with reference to Cather's correspondence all previous biographical sources in what now serves as the definitive biography.

Book-Length Critical Studies and Collections

Arnold, Marilyn. *Willa Cather: A Reference Guide.* Boston: G. K. Hall, 1986. An invaluable listing and careful commentary on Cather criticism from 1895 to 1984.

Arnold, Marilyn. *Willa Cather's Short Fiction*. Athens: Ohio University Press, 1984. The first and only book-length introduction to Cather's short stories.

Bloom, Edward A. and Lillian D. *Willa Cather's Gift of Sympathy*. Carbondale: Southern Illinois University Press, 1962. Especially valuable for Cather's literary theories and practices, and for placing her in various literary traditions.

Bloom, Harold. *Willa Cather (Modern Critical Views)*. New York: Chelsea House, 1985. Reprints articles on individual novels by Trilling, Kazin, Randall, Van Ghent, Sutherland, Welty, Murphy, and Arnold.

———. *Willa Cather's "My Ántonia" (Modern Critical Interpretations)*. New York: Chelsea House, 1987. Reprints articles on the novel by Miller, Scholes, Stegner, Martin, Stouck, Gelfant, Helmick, and Lambert.

Daiches, David. *Willa Cather: A Critical Introduction*. Ithaca, N.Y.: Cornell University Press, 1951. Concerns aesthetics, effects managed in landscapes and interiors, etc.

Fryer, Judith. *Felicitous Space: The Imaginative Structures of Edith Wharton and Willa Cather*. Chapel Hill: University of North Carolina Press, 1986. Discusses the influence on Cather of Millet and the Barbizon painters.

Gerber, Philip L. *Willa Cather*. Twayne United States Authors Series. Boston: Hall, 1975. Valuable for placing Cather in her literary milieu, although disappointing in treating individual novels.

Giannone, Richard. *Music in Willa Cather's Fiction*. Lincoln: University of Nebraska Press, 1966. Examines the novels from the perspective of musical references and structural dimensions.

Murphy, John J., ed. *Critical Essays on Willa Cather*. Boston: Hall, 1984. Includes a survey of Cather's critical reception, reprints significant essays and reviews from 1912 to the present, and contains original essays by James Woodress, David Stouck, John J. Murphy, and Paul Comeau.

O'Brien, Sharon. *Willa Cather: The Emerging Voice*. New York: Oxford, 1987. Examines Cather's masculinity as a response to patriarchal society and the effect on her fiction of her lesbian identity and relationship with her mother.

Randall, John H., III. *The Landscape and the Looking Glass: Willa Cather's Search for Value*. Boston: Houghton Mifflin, 1960. Somewhat blurred but exhaustive attempt to scrutinize the author's attitudes in relation to her time.

Rosowski, Susan J. *Approaches to Teaching Cather's "My Ántonia."* New York: Modern Language Association, 1989. A generous collection by a variety of established and new critics.

———. *The Voyage Perilous: Willa Cather's Romanticism*. Lincoln: University of Nebraska, 1986. Sees Cather in the British romantic tradition and as vindicating imaginative thought in a materialistic age.

Schroeter, James, ed. *Willa Cather and Her Critics*. Ithaca, N.Y.: Cornell University Press, 1967. A helpful if uneven gathering of general estimates by big-name critics from Mencken to Edel.

Stouck, David. *Willa Cather's Imagination*. Lincoln: University of Nebraska Press, 1975. Considers the various modes from pastoral to satiric, through which the fiction moves.

Van Ghent, Dorothy. *Willa Cather*. University of Minnesota Pamphlets on American Writers. Minneapolis: University of Minnesota Press, 1964. Assesses work in terms of the lost self and recovery of ancestors.

Critical Articles and Chapters on *My Ántonia*

Berthoff, Warner. *The Ferment of Realism: American Literature 1884–1919*, 255–63. New York: Free Press, 1965.

Bourne, Randolph. "Morals and Art from the West." *Dial* 65 (1918):557. Reprinted in *Critical Essays on Willa Cather*, 145–46.

Bowden, Edwin T. *The Dungeon of the Heart: Human Isolation and the American Novel*, 43–54. New York: Macmillan, 1961.

Charles, Isabel. "*My Ántonia*: A Dark Dimension." *Western American Literature* 2 (1967):91–108.

Selected Bibliography

Dahl, Curtis. "An American Georgic: Willa Cather's *My Ántonia*." *Comparative Literature* 7 (1955):43–51.

Erisman, Fred. "Western Regional Writers and the Uses of Place." *Journal of the West* 19 (1980):36–44.

Feger, Lois. "The Dark Dimension of Willa Cather's *My Ántonia*." *English Journal* 59 (1970):774–79.

Geismar, Maxwell. "Willa Cather: Lady in the Wilderness." In *The Last of the Provincials: The American Novel, 1915–1925*, 153–220. Boston: Houghton Mifflin, 1947. Reprinted in *Willa Cather and Her Critics*, 171–202.

Gelfant, Blanche H. "The Forgotten Reaping-hook: Sex in *My Ántonia*." *American Literature* 43 (1971):60–82. Reprinted in *Critical Essays on Willa Cather*, 147–64.

Goodman, Charlotte. "The Lost Brother, the Twin: Women Novelists and the Male–Female Double Bildungsroman." *Novel* 17 (1983):28–43.

Haller, Evelyn. "The Iconography of Vice in Willa Cather's *My Ántonia*." *Colby Library Quarterly* 14 (1978):93–102.

Harris, Richard C. "Renaissance Pastoral Conventions and the Ending of *My Ántonia*." *Markham Review* 8 (1978):8–11.

Helmick, Evelyn. "The Mysteries of Ántonia." *Midwest Quarterly* 17 (1976):173–85.

Hicks, Granville. "The Case against Willa Cather." *English Journal* 22 (1933):703–10. Reprinted in *Willa Cather and Her Critics*, 139–47.

Holman, C. Hugh. *Windows on the World: Essays on American Social Fiction*, 183–88. Knoxville: University of Tennessee Press, 1979.

Jacks, L. V. "The Classics and Willa Cather." *Prairie Schooner* 34 (1961):289–96.

Jones, Howard Mumford. "Willa Cather." In *The Frontier in American Fiction: Four Lectures on the Relation of Landscape to Literature*, 75–95. Jerusalem: Magness Press, 1956.

Kazin, Alfred. "Elegy and Satire: Willa Cather and Ellen Glasgow." In *On Native Grounds: An Interpretation of Modern American Prose Literature*, 247–64. New York: Harcourt, Brace, 1942. Reprinted in *Willa Cather and Her Critics*, 161–70.

Lambert, Deborah. "The Defeat of a Hero: Autonomy and Sexuality in *My Ántonia*." *American Literature* 53 (1982):76–90.

Martin, Terence. "The Drama of Memory in *My Ántonia*." *PMLA* 84 (1969):304–11.

Mencken, H. L. "Sunrise on the Prairie." *Smart Set* 58 (1919):143–44. Reprinted in *H. L. Mencken's "Smart Set" Criticism*, edited by William H. Nolte, 264–66. Ithaca, N.Y.: Cornell University Press, 1968.

Miller, James E., Jr. "*My Ántonia*: A Frontier Drama of Time." *American Quarterly* 10 (1958):476–84.

Murphy, John J. "Nebraska Naturalism in Jamesian Frames." *Great Plains Quarterly* 4 (1984):231–37.

———. "The Virginian and Ántonia Shimerda: Different Sides of the Western Coin." In *Women and Western American Literature,* edited by Helen Winter Stauffer and Susan J. Rosowski, 162–78. Troy: Whitston, 1982.

———. "Willa Cather and Hawthorne: Significant Resemblances." *Renascence* 27 (1975):161–75.

Olsen, Paul A. "The Epic and Great Plains Literature: Rolvaag, Cather and Neihardt." *Prairie Schooner* 55 (1981):263–85.

Popken, Randall L. "From Innocence to Experience in *My Ántonia* and Boy Life on the Prairie." *North Dakota Quarterly* 46 (1978):73–81.

Randall, John H., III. "Willa Cather and the Pastoral Tradition." In *Five Essays on Willa Cather: The Merrimack Symposium,* edited by John J. Murphy, 75–96. North Andover: Merrimack College, 1974.

Rucker, Mary E. "Prospective Focus in *My Ántonia*." *Arizona Quarterly* 29 (1973):303–16.

Scholes, Robert E. "Hope and Memory in *My Ántonia*." *Shenandoah* 14 (1962):24–29.

Sellars, Richard West. "The Interrelationship of Literature, History, and Geography in Western Living." *Western Historical Quarterly* 4 (1973):171–85.

Shaw, Patrick, W. "*My Ántonia*: Emergence and Authorial Revelations." *American Literature* 56 (1984):527–40.

Slote, Bernice. "Willa Cather: The Secret Web." In *Five Essays on Willa Cather: The Merrimack Symposium,* edited by John J. Murphy, 1–19. North Andover: Merrimack College, 1974.

Stegner, Wallace. "Willa Cather: *My Ántonia*." In *The American Novel from James Fenimore Cooper to William Faulkner,* edited by Wallace Stegner, 144–53. New York: Basic Books, 1965.

Stouck, David. "Marriage and Friendship in *My Ántonia*." *Great Plains Quarterly* 2 (1982):224–31.

Stuckey, William J. "*My Ántonia*: A Rose for Miss Cather." *Studies in the Novel* 4 (1972):473–83.

Van Doren, Carl. "Willa Cather." *Nation* 113 (1921):92–93. Revised and expanded in *Contemporary American Novelists 1900–1920,* 113–22. New York: Macmillan, 1922. Reprinted in *Willa Cather and Her Critics,* 13–19.

Wasserman, Loretta. "The Lovely Storm: Sexual Initiation in Two Early Willa Cather Novels." *Studies in the Novel* 14 (1982):348–58.

Watkins, Floyd C. "*My Ántonia*: 'Still, All Day Long Nebraska.'" In *In Time and Place: Some Origins of American Fiction*, 73–101. Athens: University of Georgia Press, 1977.

Whipple, T. K. "Willa Cather." In *Spokesmen: Modern Writers and American Life*, 139–60. New York: Appleton, 1928. Reprinted in *Willa Cather and Her Critics*, 35–51.

Index

About the Author

John J. Murphy, professor of English at Brigham Young University, is the editor of *Critical Essays on Willa Cather* (1984) and *Five Essays on Willa Cather: The Merrimack Symposium* (1974). He serves on the Board of Governors of the Willa Cather Pioneer Memorial, Red Cloud, Nebraska, and on the editorial board of *Western American Literature*. His numerous scholarly essays on Cather and other American writers have appeared in such journals as *American Literature, Prairie Schooner, Great Plains Quarterly, Thought,* and *Queen's Quarterly,* and in several volumes, including *A Literary History of the American West* (1987), *Willa Cather (Modern Critical Views)* (1985), *Fifty Western Writers* (1982), and *Women and Western American Literature* (1982). A National Endowment for the Humanities fellow in 1982 and Brigham Young's Blue Key Professor of the Year for 1986–87, Murphy contributes the "Fiction: 1900 to the 1930s" essay to the bibliographical annual *American Literary Scholarship.*